# LIGHTING THE PATH

With very best wishes, Maia.
May your path be joyful!

# LIGHTING THE PATH

*A guide to using and understanding the I Ching, or Book of Changes, the ancient and wonderful Chinese oracle.*

**Nigel Peace**

Nigel Peace © 2012

All rights reserved

No parts of this publication may be reproduced, stored in a retrieval system, or transmitted in any form or by any means whatsoever without the prior permission of the publisher.

A record of this publication is available from the British Library.

ISBN 978-1-907203-26-8

Published by Local Legend
*www.local-legend.co.uk*

Cover design by Titanium Design Ltd
*www.titaniumdesign.co.uk*

Printed by Lightning Source UK
*www.lightningsource.com*

Typesetting by Wordzworth Ltd
*www.wordzworth.com*

Cover photograph by Sylvie Gotti

The Ba-Gua diagram is by the author

*In loving memory of and gratitude to
King Wen and Richard Wilhelm,
and all the many other kind souls who brought
the beautiful work of the I Ching to the world.*

### The author

Nigel Peace has more than thirty years experience of using the I Ching to receive guidance for himself and others. He gives personal consultations, lectures and workshops on the subject, demystifying it with down-to-earth language.

### His other books include:

5P1R1T R3V3L4T10N5

A description of provably precognitive dreams and synchronicities, written to encourage all those trying to live a more meaningful and spiritual life that each of us can receive genuine guidance in the everyday world. The book was voted second in The People's Book Prize national awards.

51GN5 OF L1F3

A comedy fantasy novel of the afterlife, written to suggest that not everything in Heaven and Earth should be taken too seriously.

*www.local-legend.co.uk*
*www.spiritrevelations.com*

# Contents

| | |
|---|---|
| Introduction: The Purpose of this Book | 1 |
| The Development of the I Ching | 15 |
| The Trigrams | 27 |
| Forming Your Question | 37 |
| Methods for Consulting the I Ching | 47 |
|     The Yarrow Stalks Method | 50 |
|     The Marbles Method | 51 |
|     The Coins Method | 52 |
|     The Playing Cards Method | 53 |
|     Personalised Methods | 53 |
| How to Do a Reading | 57 |
| Examples of I Ching Readings | 71 |
| Appendix A    On Probabilities | 151 |
| Appendix B    The I Ching's Attitude to this Book | 161 |
| Appendix C    A Glossary of Words and Phrases | 165 |
| Bibliography | 175 |

# Introduction:
# The Purpose of this Book

The I Ching is a collection of oracles originating in China more than four thousand years ago. In the course of its development, it has become a source of practical and spiritual guidance, both extraordinarily accurate and humanely wise, that is as relevant and meaningful today as at any time in its history. It stands head and shoulders above virtually all other systems of divination for another two reasons:

- It does not merely describe in detail the inner reality of the situations facing us, and nor does it merely offer predictions about their likely outcomes, but it actually *empowers* us in our own destinies by offering us choices of action and attitude.
- We do not need the services of the holy man or seer – *anyone* can learn how to use this Book [1] for themselves.

---

1  It is a small idiosyncrasy of mine to use a capital letter here, as a sign of my deep respect for the I Ching.

With over thirty years experience of using the I Ching both for myself and to help others, I still never fail to be astonished by its responses and have never been let down when following its advice. Several true examples will be given in this book so that you may judge for yourself. Therefore, I want to bring the I Ching to a wider audience and to encourage those who know little or nothing about it to use it for themselves. Like any esoteric practice, however, there is a certain air of mystery about the Book that puts some people off. I am going to try and reassure you that there is no need for this: it is not a religious book, it contains no doctrines or articles of faith that must be adopted, and it is written for *everyone* to use and to share.

> *There is nothing like the feeling of inner strength that comes from knowing that one is never alone and that at any time one can access genuine and loving guidance in one's difficulties.*

But it also has to be said that some people who do begin to use the I Ching have some initial difficulties. These may concern the best method to be used, the phrasing of the question one is going to ask guidance on, or the interpretation of the response. It is true that the original language [2] of the Book seems rather archaic to us at times. Therefore I also want to offer a humble lending hand to those of you who already have some experience in consulting the I Ching but who may sometimes feel a little confused.

The following sections, then, give a brief history of the Book and a description of its structure; there is then advice on how to form your question and how to carry out a consultation, with several alternative methods offered so that you can choose the one that feels right for you. Most importantly, there are lots of real examples given so that you may get a good feel for the spirit with which the Book speaks, and a

---

2  The Bibliography lists several alternative translations.

comprehensive glossary of words and phrases often used, to help with your interpretations.

Life can be pretty tough these days, especially for the very many people who are sincerely trying to follow a more meaningful and spiritual path.

We seem to be beset by increasingly complicated and demanding challenges, with financial and working-life issues, the stress of travel in busy towns and cities, an information and communications overload from the media and the Internet. There don't seem to be enough hours in the day and we never seem to get enough proper rest. Both psychologically and emotionally, we probably demand more of ourselves and of our relationships with others than any generation before us, intent on inner peace and mutual understanding, the pursuit of happiness and of personal fulfilment.

And if all this were not enough, there is the call of the spirit. With social and political systems, not to mention the Earth herself, seemingly in crisis, we yearn for the reality of the promised New Age, a time when the world and its peoples are governed by principles of love, caring and compassion.

We frequently find ourselves facing important decisions and challenges, from the purely practical to the emotional and moral.

- My job is frustrating so should I change it?
- I've just met someone I like but are they good for me?
- How should I deal with my nuisance neighbours or my bullying boss?
- I feel unhappy in my relationship – where is it going?
- What can I do to feel more secure?
- How can I be of more service to others?

But we want to know not just what we *can* do in the circumstances, but moreover what is *the right thing* to do. By this is meant that it is often not enough to discern a solution or a course of action that simply serves our immediate interests. Those who are truly on the spiritual path will wish to find an answer that is 'in harmony with natural law', a way of being that understands others' concerns as well as our own, a solution that is creative and life-affirming, that addresses our long-term personal growth as human beings. We want a source of wisdom that can tell the difference between what is *really* important and what in the great scheme of things just isn't. We want, like Saint Francis, to know what can be changed and what isn't worth worrying about!

When we feel a bit lost on our personal journey and in need of some good advice, where can we turn? If our issue is related to our physical or psychological health, there are of course doctors, counsellors and psychotherapists who have specialist skills and access to relevant information. When we seek a more psychic or esoteric solution, perhaps a glimpse into the future, we may turn to a clairvoyant or seer, an astrologer or Tarot reader. There is now any number of New Age teachers and workshop gurus who can help us to learn new skills, such as healing, or new ways of thinking that will encourage our development. More prosaically, but no less important, when we have a personal issue there is no substitute for a wise mother or a very good friend!

But what if these people are not available, or we do not have access to them because of financial or other circumstances? Moreover – and herein lies the real point – there are two other pretty significant questions:

- How do we know that we can trust the information or advice given?
- What can we do with the information anyway?

## LIGHTING THE PATH

When we are seeking 'information' of any kind, we have become accustomed to getting it from *someone else*, be that a doctor or a guru, an author or the Internet. This is partly because, of course, there is so much specialised knowledge in the human world now that we cannot possibly expect to know everything ourselves, or even all those things that are relevant to us. Another reason is that we have actively been taught, through formal education, that knowledge is the preserve of 'experts'. This is true, up to a point. In no way do I wish to imply that genuine experts in their own fields should not deserve our respect. [3]

But do we always know with complete confidence that the source we are addressing is a genuinely expert one? Even scientists who have brought us many fabulous advances in medicine and technology, for example, readily admit that their knowledge is very imperfect. The point is that such knowledge is merely *information* and not 'The Truth'. Moreover, that information is very often founded upon theories and assumptions and beliefs that may in the course of time be shown to be false. And as for the information sourced from the Internet, where absolutely anyone is freely able to post their purely personal assertions......

When it comes to more personal guidance, rather than answers to technical questions, we face even greater problems of trust! Nowadays there is, unfortunately, an overloaded and creaking bandwagon of New Age writers and teachers [4], all jostling for your attention, your faith and your money. Many of them are well-meaning, and a proportion of these do indeed have valuable insight and experience to share. Some are frankly self-seeking charlatans making wild assertions appar-

---

[3] Nor am I going to suggest that one might consult the I Ching on a question such as "What shall I do about this purple rash on my leg?"
[4] I am one of them. However, I do not claim to be an 'expert' on the I Ching, for there are many who will know its history and structure in greater detail. This book is about how to use it, quite a different skill.

ently channelled from extraterrestrial intelligences yet offering not a shred of evidence of their veracity. Careful judgement must be used in deciding which is which. But again, the guidance received from even the genuine advisor – be that a seer, a psychic or a faithful friend – is substantially coloured by that person's belief system. No human being can know The Truth, and we are well advised to run fast in the opposite direction from anyone who claims to.

So there is an issue of trust regarding the source of information or guidance that we may seek. Suppose that we can overcome this, either by being satisfied as to the advisor's credentials or simply by being prepared to keep an open mind, there is still the question of how *useful* the information really is. Let us say that we go to a clairvoyant or Tarot reader, for example, who tells us that a wonderful opportunity will present itself next year, or we shall meet someone important, or unexpectedly receive money. This might lift our spirits momentarily but there is absolutely nothing that we can do about such scenarios except sit back and see what happens. All too often, there is an implicit assumption in matters of divination that there is some fixed sort of destiny at work in our lives and all we have to do is wait for the waves to break on the shoreline of our daily life. In other words, the course of our lives has very little to do with us. Insofar as we go along with this way of thinking, we have only ourselves to blame for our feelings of loneliness and impotence, for the sadness of our circumstances and the cruelty of Fate [5].

> *If we neglect our own responsibility for the course of our lives, and surrender our power to others – however expert, however wise, however experienced*

---

[5] I shall use the word 'fate' to mean a fixed outcome that we can do nothing to alter, whereas 'destiny' is a natural flow or rhythm to our lives that may have a certain probability but which we can consciously influence.

# LIGHTING THE PATH

> *– then we can expect no personal growth and we shall never know what it is to be truly human.*

This, I suggest, is central to the philosophy of the I Ching. There is only one true source of guidance. It is the greatest source possible and the most trustworthy, that knows you and your needs and concerns better than anyone else possibly could, that loves you unconditionally and has only your best interests at heart the whole time, day and night, twenty-four-seven. It is YOU, your highest self, your own deepest and unconscious mind. Some call it the soul.

In ancient times, the unseen energies determining the ups and downs of our lives, and of the natural world, were thought of as gods and demons, ghosts and ancestors and nature spirits. In China these were called 'shen' and indeed the first authors of the I Ching described life in these terms. So uncannily accurate was the oracle in describing the transformations brought about by the unseen world that many believed the Book itself to be 'inhabited' by spirits. Even today, unfortunately, there are still those who prefer to attribute their negative experiences to malicious or possessive spirits, and to petition guides and angels to bring about the positive. But our lives are only meaningful and purposeful, surely, insofar as we accept our own responsibility for their development. The I Ching has itself developed in the course of history to reflect this. Its shamanic authors recognised the essential and universal factors at work in human situations, and encoded them in an archetypal symbolism that is as true for us today as it was in ancient times. Thus it doesn't matter whether we think of those factors as external spirits or inner psychological drivers; what matters is that we actively work with them.

When consulting the I Ching, we open a doorway to the deepest mind, or soul. Somewhere in the unconscious, your mind knows with great clarity what the *real* issues are in your situation, the underlying forces at work shaping your experiences. It also knows what are the options available to you in dealing with it, as well as how they are likely to turn out (because we store vast amounts of information in the unconscious, derived every day from our senses both physical and esoteric). We have all experienced at least the occasional night-time dream in which our minds seem to be telling us something important that we need to know but are not aware of – or are deliberately shutting out – when awake. The I Ching is a tool, if you like, that we can use deliberately in waking life for the same purpose. In its pages we read a description of those unseen forces, and our options are reflected back to us. Thus we are invited to take responsibility in shaping our own destiny. We reclaim our power.

You may be thinking that this is all pretty high-flown and mystical stuff that has little to do with everyday down-to-earth life. Not a bit of it. Your soul knows very well that you are living an utterly material life too, and if you don't get that sorted then what chance have you got of any spiritual development? Your home life, your job, your relationships and your finances, or your lack of any of these, are hugely important to you and all such things impact on your personal growth just as much as the deep moral issues of life and the heart-wrenching emotional troubles. The I Ching is a *practical* book.

Here's an example. I was taught the use of the I Ching by a respected China scholar who was quite tough on me, I'm now glad to say. He insisted on proper preparation and considerable thought being given to the question asked (in order to be clear that it *was* the right question). Nonetheless, almost the first time I used the Book for myself I thought I must have done something wrong, so dramatic and improbable was the response.

# LIGHTING THE PATH

At that time I was a young school teacher, with a wife and a child and very little money. So I applied for a promotion at a different school. The interview went well and I was offered the job, and I asked for a day to think it over. I had no reason, consciously at least, to think that anything might be amiss but I wanted to consult the I Ching about my prospects. My question was "Will this new job be successful for me?" and the result was as follows.

Hexagram 62 : Preponderance of the Small<br>(with 1st, 3rd, 4th and 6th lines moving) [6]

This chapter describes an exceptional situation of struggle in which one is only able to achieve small things and has to adopt a conscientious and very modest attitude. One must attend simply to one's duty and not try to stand out in any way. It did not seem very auspicious!

But it got even worse. When one looks at the specific 'moving lines' (these draw our attention to particularly important aspects of the situation), there is further reference to the need for extreme reticence and self-control, and to the possibility of actual personal danger and perhaps attack, misfortune and injury. Hmmm, surely this would be enough to put anyone off?

However, note that the Book is *not* saying "You should not take this job". What it has done so far is to describe some underlying (certainly hidden) forces at play in this situation, at the school, that would have an impact on the way I went about my work there. I was being told that it would be a difficult experience, yet the decision is still left up to me. Certainly, there are many times in our lives when we are faced with challenges that we honestly don't feel up to just then, or are even genuinely to be avoided. There's no shame in that. But this doesn't mean that we should always reject

---

[6] The terms 'Hexagram' and 'moving lines' will be explained a little later.

difficult challenges, for often they can be the source of great achievements.

This is where the I Ching really comes into its own, because its response doesn't stop at this point (as a conventional fortune-teller might). Having taken notice of the moving lines we are then directed to a new hexagram, or chapter, which describes the likely outcome of the situation, *given that we have understood and accepted the personal message for us in the initial reading.* Now, at that time of my life I had a rather forceful and determined personality; I was ambitious both to progress personally and to educate my pupils well in my subject. So far I had been told that I would have seriously to reign in that personality and not expect great educational achievements (quite apart from the other rather dark warnings). Was I prepared for that? The chapter describing outcome was Hexagram 27 : Nourishment.

The things that we need for our personal nourishment are very varied, from food and drink to others' love and recognition, from physical pleasures to spiritual growth. The hexagram describes the importance of each of these, as well as nourishment in the sense of caring for others. This was entirely appropriate to my situation in several ways, for on the one hand I needed the money of this promotion to support my family while on the other hand I cared about my own and my pupils' development. But the hexagram has two further things to say. Firstly, there is the suggestion that we carefully observe the other people around us and how they choose to 'nourish' themselves, for this tells us much about their true nature. Secondly, there is the advice, entirely in keeping with the initial reading, that we should try to achieve inner tranquillity so that the ways in which we express ourselves are not 'excessive'. This has a pretty direct resonance for a school teacher!

## LIGHTING THE PATH

What I understood from this consultation, then, was that if I accepted the job offer I would be in for quite a tough time. I would need to be very careful in the relationships I formed and in the ways I expressed myself. I could not expect personal advancement, or much response from my pupils. *On the other hand*, if I could deal with it properly, it would be a situation of considerable nourishment for me in the sense of character development.

Would you have accepted the job?

Well, my financial situation was dire and in those early days I did not yet know to what extent I could trust the I Ching anyway, so I did accept it. I then embarked on a year and a half of torment and stress. In ways that I couldn't possibly have foreseen at the time of my interview, it turned out to be an awful school with weak management, low standards and few resources. As the youngest teacher, I was assigned the lowest-achieving classes with the most challenging behaviour. There were barely half a dozen text books available, and those were in poor condition. When there were problems (almost daily) there was little or no support from either senior teachers or parents. In often inflammatory situations, I quickly learned to bite my lip and review my expectations. I suffered theft, vandalism to my car and I was once actually physically attacked by a pupil.

However, I really did learn how to control that 'forceful personality' and I really learned how to teach and how to control a classroom. As a bonus, the teaching materials I had had to write for my pupils were later published as a book, which brought in extra money. And I eventually applied successfully for a new job at a wonderful school, where I stayed happily for nearly thirty years and where my previous tough experience was a major factor in my being accepted.

How did a Chinese book over four thousand years old know all that?

Of course, *it* didn't. But somehow, somewhere in my deepest unconscious mind, *I* knew it. And as I have said, the I Ching is a tool with which we can deliberately bring forth that 'higher information' into our everyday awareness. How this could be so is, I believe, one of the greatest questions facing human beings for it is absolutely central to our understanding of the nature of consciousness (not to mention that of time). The clear implication is that our minds are incredibly powerful and that we have access to knowledge far beyond the use of the physical senses. Moreover, we can see the future in some detail.

Isn't this exciting?!

LIGHTING THE PATH

## Summary

- This book is meant to be used as a companion to the I Ching, to guide the reader in choosing a good method of consultation, phrasing the question to be asked and interpreting the response. It is intended both for complete beginners and for those with some experience.
- The I Ching is a method of divination offering guidance in life's challenges, whether these are practical, emotional, moral or spiritual. It helps us know what 'the right thing to do' is.
- When we seek advice from others, we do not really know whether we can trust the information given. The I Ching helps us to access the highest source of advice possible, our own deepest mind.
- The I Ching not only uncovers the hidden forces shaping our situation, it is unique in also advising us how we can approach the coming changes and in suggesting the likely outcomes of our actions and attitudes. It empowers us in shaping our own destiny.
- A consultation can reveal information completely unknown to our conscious mind, including accurate information about events in the future.

# The Development of the I Ching

This is just a brief outline of the Book's origins, so that one may begin to appreciate better its purposes and structure; in turn, this may help the reader with interpreting its responses.

The essential theme of the Book is that all life is undergoing constant change and transformation according to natural rhythms, just like the seasons of the year, and that understanding how these work in our everyday lives helps us to make better decisions. The word 'I' (pronounced 'ee') means both change and our responses to it. But there are also many other forces at work shaping these patterns, factors arising from our own previous experiences, the impulses of our own personalities and characters that incline us towards one action or reaction or another. And this is not even to mention the impulses and inclinations of the other people who share our lives, both known and presently unknown to us.

We are often quite unaware of these underlying energies. There are so many factors at play shaping any situation we may find ourselves in and most of them are entirely beyond our influence or control. People are especially unpredictable! Even if we are in a relationship with someone, whether it is a friend or a lover or a work colleague, we can never quite predict how they are going to respond to what we say or do or to what is going on around us. However well we know someone, we cannot know everything about their past and what's going through their mind. In fact, most of the time we know very little indeed. We know even less, of course, about what's going through the minds of people whom we don't know but who are affecting, or are about to affect, our situation.

Consider for example the case of someone who is unhappy at work and feels that their contribution is not being properly recognised. The first thing to take into account is their own ambitions and expectations, the pressures they may feel under as a result of their upbringing or their current family and financial situation. Now extend exactly the same considerations to their work colleagues, including the management, and we recognise that there is a complex of psychological and emotional factors that might contribute to personal tensions and differences of opinion and intention. So far we haven't even mentioned spirituality, and individuals' desire for meaningful and ethical interactions and productive outcomes. Now let's include the external factors such as market forces, the company's economic circumstances, and its leaders' plans and ability to carry them out... most if not all of which our original unhappy worker will be entirely ignorant of. There is a huge number of potential reasons for that unhappiness, and our hero has to get to the bottom of those before any decisions can be taken to improve matters.

So the first task of the I Ching when we consult it is to describe these hidden energies. This might confirm our own intuition, or at least make perfect sense to us, or it might be very surprising.

Secondly, the Book's philosophy is one of *change*. Nothing is ever static. However stuck a situation seems to be, there will eventually be movement and a transformation into something new. This is because our own life's energies, just like the natural world, follow patterns and rhythms. For example, I once consulted the I Ching about the future of a relationship that was important to me but seemed to be failing and there seemed to be nothing I could do about it: I obtained the result 'Breakthrough', which is self-explanatory, and so it proved. (Incidentally, the very next day I heard a radio play in which a character consulted the I Ching on a similar question and obtained exactly the same result! Such synchronicity demonstrates that we are indeed bringing some kind of awareness from our higher mind into our everyday consciousness when we use the Book.)

However, I repeat that the Book is *not* about fortune-telling. It absolutely does *not* believe in predestination. Yes, there are forces at work shaping our circumstances and sometimes these are very powerful, but there is always something that we can do about it – even if that is just to be better prepared and to adopt a different attitude of mind. Therefore the I Ching will offer us advice about how to approach our situation and what actions might be taken that would be wise and moral. In other words, it *empowers* us in our own destiny. Certainly, there might occasionally be periods in life when, just as in winter, nothing seems to be moving or growing, and circumstances (maybe other people too) are against us. The Book might then counsel us that to take action could be pointless or even dangerous, and that we must 'retreat' and maintain our personal integrity; on the other hand, we will be assured that the situation must change, and there could be specific clues given as to how this will happen.

One of the Book's later authors was Confucius, the Chinese sage of around 500 BC. He said: "Everything flows on and on like the river, without pause, day and night." Nothing is ever still. What we see in our lives is mostly the surface, the eddies and ripples, the turbulence over the rocks and perhaps the majesty of the waterfall. But underneath all that are the currents and powerful energies. Beneath the individual and transitory things of life, there are eternal natural laws at work. (This is the philosophy of Taoism.)

In ancient China, in the days of hunting and gathering before recorded history, people felt themselves to be very much at the mercy of hidden forces. They knew little about those 'eternal natural laws' yet they still understood, or at least their shamanic leaders did, that there were rhythms and patterns in life's energy and that it would be best to work with these rather than in ignorance of them. The predominant impulse for these people was simple survival. So they sought a means of magically connecting with these forces – a system of divination that would guide their behaviour.

The earliest references to the Book credit Fu Hsi, the first of the 'Three Noble Emperors' born in 2852 BC, with inventing the first 'kua' (or 'gua') or linear signs, as a method of fortune-telling. Essentially, ——— meant 'yes' and — — meant 'no'. This was pretty basic stuff, yet with its origins in quite sophisticated metaphysics. Every human civilisation has asked itself "Where do we come from? What is the origin of all things?" For the Chinese, the primal creative force of the universe, from which all life develops, was represented by a single solid line ——— which was called t'ai chi ('the ridgepole', since it is this that forms the essential support of a dwelling). This sign represents indivisible unity, strength and the Heavenly world. But simultaneously it also implies the duality of the material world, or Earthly life; there is an 'above' the line and a 'below' the line, and moreover it is from one's dwelling that one emerges into the world. The One gives life to the Two, as the forces of Heaven create life on Earth. But then a second sign was needed to physically represent the human world, hence the line was drawn broken into two parts — — . The solid line represented the powerful and 'positive' energy of the unseen mystical world, while the broken line represented the yielding and 'negative' energy of human life [7].

But as a system of divination, this was far too simplistic. So then these lines were added together to represent more varied answers such as "yes but…" and "well, yes and no" and "no just for the moment" and so on. At first there were pairs of lines ('young, stable' yes and no, and 'old, changing' yes and no) and by the time of the Hsia Dynasty around 2,200 BC we had groups of three lines forming what we now call trigrams. These have been found inscribed upon pieces of bone or on stones and clearly used as an oracle; they are perhaps the origin of Chinese pictographic script.

What do they mean? Well, there are eight possible arrangements of three lines, and by this time the thinking about them was becoming quite subtle and advanced. For one thing, according to one modern translation, they were thought of as "images of all that happens in Heaven and on Earth". This is a very bold step. Each trigram had an 'attribute' such as Strength, Danger or Joy and an associated 'image' such as Thunder, Mountain or Fire. They also represented the traditional responsibilities, duties and characteristics of each member of a family: a father, mother, three sons and three daughters.

But the really important step forward – and this is the key to the Book - is that these images were not thought of as static, but representing states of being that are continuously in transition, or 'moving natural processes'. Any one of the lines could be regarded as in a state of movement, so that it might change into its opposite ('yes' into 'no' if you like), and

---

[7] Note that the word 'negative' is not to be understood here as 'a bad thing', rather it is simply one essential part of life's polarity. Just as there is light and there is dark, each is in balance with the other and indeed depends upon it. These are ways of describing duality and are not moral judgements.

therefore one trigram could change into a different one, just as phenomena of the real world are also always changing.

We see this right from the beginning in the structure of the trigrams themselves. For example, here are the three 'sons' showing how the father's strength (the unbroken line) is represented in the sons: it begins to move, then passes through action and danger to a state of rest and completion [8].

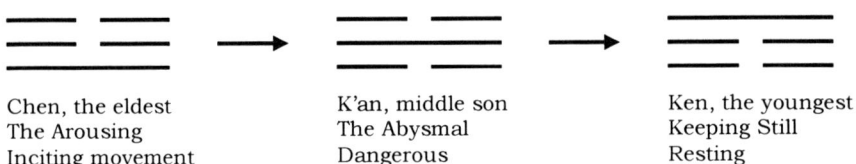

Chen, the eldest
The Arousing
Inciting movement

K'an, middle son
The Abysmal
Dangerous

Ken, the youngest
Keeping Still
Resting

Now, what would you do with yourself if you were imprisoned by a tyrant for a long period in solitary confinement? Well, you'd probably feel a bit sorry for yourself. You might read a few books, if you were allowed to. You'd probably scratch a few marks on the wall of your cell. But not King Wen. He was a strong and wise leader who sought an agreement with his people's enemy Chou Hsin in about 1150 BC, but was instead held in captivity for seven years, his own forces not yet strong enough to release him. He passed the time of his incarceration by creating the most extraordinary and brilliant system of divination in history. He is the father of the I Ching as we know it today. The first thing he did was to combine pairs of trigrams with each other to represent a greater variety of transformative influences, the fullest range of contrasts; these sixty-four 'hexagrams' were now thought to represent *"every possible fundamental and typical human situation"*.

For example, Hexagram 2 is called The Receptive. It is a doubling of the 'mother' trigram and represents an archetypal

---

8   We'll come to the question of how the lines change when we look at the methods used for consulting the oracle.

state of devotion and of yielding. In the natural world, it also represents the life forces of the Earth at rest in the autumn.

Now, if the first (the lowest) line of the hexagram *moves* and changes into its opposite, we get Hexagram 24, called The Return, or Turning Point. The lower trigram now shows the first son, Chen, who arouses new energy and movement within and below the Earth, who is shown by the upper trigram, the mother.

So this new situation represents in nature the winter solstice, the turning point of the year when light begins to grow after a period of darkness. But of course this also resonates with familiar periods in everyday human life, when we pass through times of trouble and apparent stagnation towards a new time of growing hope and relief from our difficulties. [It would be nice to think, wouldn't it, that King Wen might have drawn this particular oracle for himself in his prison cell.]

> *Thus we are seeing a system of divination develop that not only represents archetypal human experiences in symbolic form, but also links them in a continuum, showing how one can move and be transformed into another.*

King Wen did much more for us than just expand the system from eight to sixty-four kua. He also began to write the descriptions of what each situation represents, both in terms of the natural rhythms of life and of human concerns, as the example above demonstrates. Moreover, it occurred to him – and this really *is* the Turning Point – that it was not enough for someone to be presented with an analysis of what's going on, like the fortune-teller mentioned earlier who might tell us that "something is going to change soon". What someone really needs is some advice about how to deal with that change, what attitude of mind to adopt, what actions can be taken so that *we go with the natural flow of life's energies*. In this way, things will automatically work out in our best interests. King Wen started this work. He was duly released, and it then fell to his son Wu, the founder of the Chou (or Zhou) Dynasty, to write the text that accompanies each of the lines in each of the hexagrams. The work now became a book of *wisdom*, complete with practical and spiritual guidance, which *empowers* one with a role in shaping one's own destiny. At this time its title was 'Chou I', meaning life's changes according to the kings of Chou.

Remember, this was over three thousand years ago. Six hundred years later, the great philosopher Confucius studied the Book intensely and added commentaries and edits, and it was his pupils who later developed the so-called 'Ten Wings' literature of the Book describing its inner meanings and philosophy in detail, and spreading its use widely. Fifty years before Confucius, the Book inspired many of Li Erh's (known as Lao Tzu) profound teachings on Taoism; and in the later Han Dynasty, all these writings were collected together as the first among the Five Classics and the Book was renamed I Ching.

But you know how it is. We humans have an unerring knack of ruining anything good that comes along, especially if we don't really understand it. Certain people can't resist demolishing great reputations, and when our energy is low we focus on the utterly trivial, like our modern celebrity culture, and publicity is splashed on anything superficially attractive and sexy however shallow. Likewise, the use of the I Ching began to deteriorate into a quick-fix and simple fortune-telling tool. Strangely, to our eyes, this was largely the fault of Tsou Yen in the fourth century BC, who introduced a superficial focus on the concept of 'yin and yang'.

Nowadays we think of this as typically Chinese, but the concept was also in widespread use elsewhere. Remember, the Chinese idea of the primal force was the single line, t'ai chi. However, in other Asian cultures such as Japan, the beginning was represented by a circle which then divided into two parts, each moving into the other.

To Chinese thinking, yin meant 'cloudy or overcast' while yang meant 'banners waving in the sun', and the image adopted was that of a mountain whose northern side is dark and whose southern side is bathed in sunlight. This is the sense in which yin and yang should be understood when using the I Ching. The idea that the two parts represent female and male characteristics is more of a Western construct with sexual overtones, added later. In any event, the focus on these ideas only seemed to lead to a more trivial and magical attitude to the Book. Its use as a source of philosophical wisdom was not fully restored until several centuries later, and it was finally consolidated into the book we know today in the Sung Period of about one thousand years ago (when the Coins Method of consultation was also introduced).

A first attempt at an English translation was made in the nineteenth century but this was largely intended as a historical document and little heed was paid to the Book's mystical philosophy and purposes. Most serious students of the Book now agree that the very best Western translation is that by Richard Wilhelm, a German scholar of Chinese language and culture who lived there for many years. Aided by his teacher Lao Nai-hsuan, the job took him ten years and was completed in 1923. The great psychiatrist Dr Carl Jung described this work as grasping "the living meaning of the text". It was he who then asked his American student Cary F Baynes to render the translation into English. It was a tough job, interrupted by world politics. She eventually finished it in 1949, helped by Wilhelm's son Hellmut, and it was first published in England in 1951 with a Foreword by Dr Jung himself. Since then there have been several other versions in English, some of them new translations and some of them reinterpretations of the concepts; but while their language is more modern and comprehensible, somehow (it seems to me) they do not quite represent the Book's true spirit in the same depth as Wilhelm.

Well, what is that true spirit? Carl Jung was a man who chose his words very carefully, so what did he mean by referring to "the living meaning of the text"? It has been said that the I Ching can touch our very soul, as if it were indeed somehow inhabited by spirits. Even to us, today, a consultation can feel like talking to a kind and wise old teacher who really knows and cares for us. This book has a living spirit of its own. Carl Jung used it himself frequently over the course of half a century, and described the results as always consistent and meaningful. Indeed, he wrote in the Foreword to Wilhelm's translation, if a human being had given him the same replies to his questions, "...I should, as a psychiatrist, have had to pronounce him of sound mind...[and] I should have had to congratulate this hypothetical person on the extent of his insight..."

# LIGHTING THE PATH

## Summary

- The philosophy of the I Ching is that life is undergoing continuous change, due to both natural rhythms of energy and also many external factors unknown to us. However, the unconscious mind can access information about these changes.
- In ancient China, a simple form of divination was used involving just two graphic symbols, a line and a broken line, to represent the positive and the negative.
- About 4,000 years ago, these lines were grouped into sets of three, called trigrams. Each had its own name, attribute and image, and also represented the relative positions of members of a family. They are symbols of archetypal experiences in human life.
- 3,000 years ago, King Wen grouped pairs of these into hexagrams, thought to represent "every possible fundamental and typical human situation". He wrote descriptions of their meanings, and his son Wu added detailed guidance to accompany each line. The Book was then called Chou I.
- Confucius and his disciples greatly extended the commentaries and other writings about the Book. It was also a major influence in Taoism.
- About 200 BC, all the writings of the Book were collected together and renamed I Ching, the first of the Five Classics of Chinese literature.
- The first true Western translation was made in German by Richard Wilhelm in 1923, and an English version of this published in 1951 by Cary F Baynes with a Foreword by Dr Carl Jung expressing great respect for the work.

# The Trigrams

It has been said that the eight trigrams were thought of as "images of all that happens in Heaven and on Earth" (Wilhelm, the Introduction). But they are states in continuous transition, changing one into another as phenomena in the real world also change. They represent the ways in which the moving rhythms of nature bring change into our lives.

It is helpful also to think of them as representing the positions, duties and functions of members of a family: father, mother, three sons and three daughters – for it is the children who carry forward the attributes of the parents. Each one has individual attributes (forms of action) and images; they have also been associated with compass directions, colours, seasons of the year, parts of the body, different kinds of feelings and so on. In these ways they provide a complete description of human experience, in both the spiritual and the material worlds.

In order to understand an I Ching reading fully, it is important to have a grasp of the basic meanings of the individual trigrams and the effects of their attributes being linked together.

This is named Ch'ien, or *The Creative*. He is the father of the trigram family and master of the spiritual, or Heavenly, world. Formed entirely of strong or 'yang' lines, he is dynamic and his attributes are creativity and enduring strength.

*Chen*, or *The Arousing*, is the family's first son. Notice that the 'masculine' or yang line is in the first (lowest) position here. To a traditional way of thinking, the role of the first son is to represent the father, to carry forward his energy into the world. So Chen's attribute is to excite or initiate activity, to make things begin, perhaps to expose what has previously been hidden. His image, unsurprisingly, is thunder.

The yang line now moves to the second position, representing the second son, *K'an*. When boys become young men and go into the world, making things happen, their energy can be powerful but also somewhat risky. There is an air of danger about K'an whose name translates unflatteringly as *The Abysmal*. This is meant in the sense of rushing water that flows on wherever it wills, overcoming obstacles without stopping.

With experience of life, the sons' strong energy gains maturity. *Ken*, the third son with a yang line in the third position, is called *Keeping Still*. He brings things to completion, clarifying what has been achieved. His attribute is resting and his image is the mountain, still and powerful.

## LIGHTING THE PATH

*K'un, The Receptive,* is the family's mother. She is composed entirely of broken or 'yin' lines. Note that while an unbroken line is thought of as 'strong', it would be misleading to think of its opposite as 'weak' in the normal sense. The mother's role in a family (to traditional thinking) is every bit as important and powerful as the father's, but in a different sense! Her strength is to accept Earthly life for what it is, to be yielding and let things pass that are not important, to be devoted to what is good for the whole family. While others are 'out making things happen', she perseveres in keeping the home together, for that is the security that everyone else falls back on.

The mother's primary representative in the world is her first daughter, *Sun.* The yin line is in the first position here. She brings the attributes of devotion and perseverance into the world in a quiet way; her name means *The Gentle* and she moves like a penetrating wind, calmly dissolving troubles as the wind moves away the clouds. Her image is sometimes also that of wood, because her younger sister depends on her...

*Li* is the second daughter, with a yin line in the second position. As the mother's persevering energy takes hold in the world through Sun's gentle action, clarity of understanding and the warmth of human relationship arise. Li's name translates as *The Clinging,* for her image is that of fire, which depends upon wood for it to burn. This fire brings light and warmth, and enables nourishment to be provided to people.

☷ As this gentle warmth penetrates human experience, the 'feminine' energy now moves to the third position, representing the youngest daughter *Tui*. She is *The Joyous*, for the ultimate expression of this soft yet strong energy is human joy; her image is that of a calm lake, a beautiful state of being yet with powerful depth.

Notice again how it can be seen, in the positions of the lines within the trigrams, that there is a *movement* of the attributes of 'father' and 'mother' in the trigrams representing the 'children'. The sons show *strength* beginning to move, passing through action and risk to rest and completion of movement; the daughters show *devotion* moving from gentle penetration, through clarity and adaptability, to joyfulness and tranquillity.

One must take care not to think of these various attributes and symbols in any superficial way as, for example, suggesting typically 'masculine' and 'feminine' characteristics. Every man must sometimes be persevering and gentle, and of course there will be times when a woman must act decisively. The images are intended to represent the whole range of human expression. Perhaps it is helpful, instead, to think of the male trigrams as representing the use of 'reason' while the female ones express 'emotion'. We all need to live with both mind and heart.

The entire family of trigrams has often been shown in the diagram below, based on the Later Heaven Arrangement, ascribed to King Wen.

# LIGHTING THE PATH

**NORTH**
Kan
6
Career
The ears
Water
Black

**Ch'ien**
1
Father, Support
The head
Heaven
White

**Ken**
7
Knowledge
The hands
Mountain
Black, blue, green

**WEST**
Tui
2
Children
The mouth
Lake
White

**Ba-Gua**

**The Trigram Family**

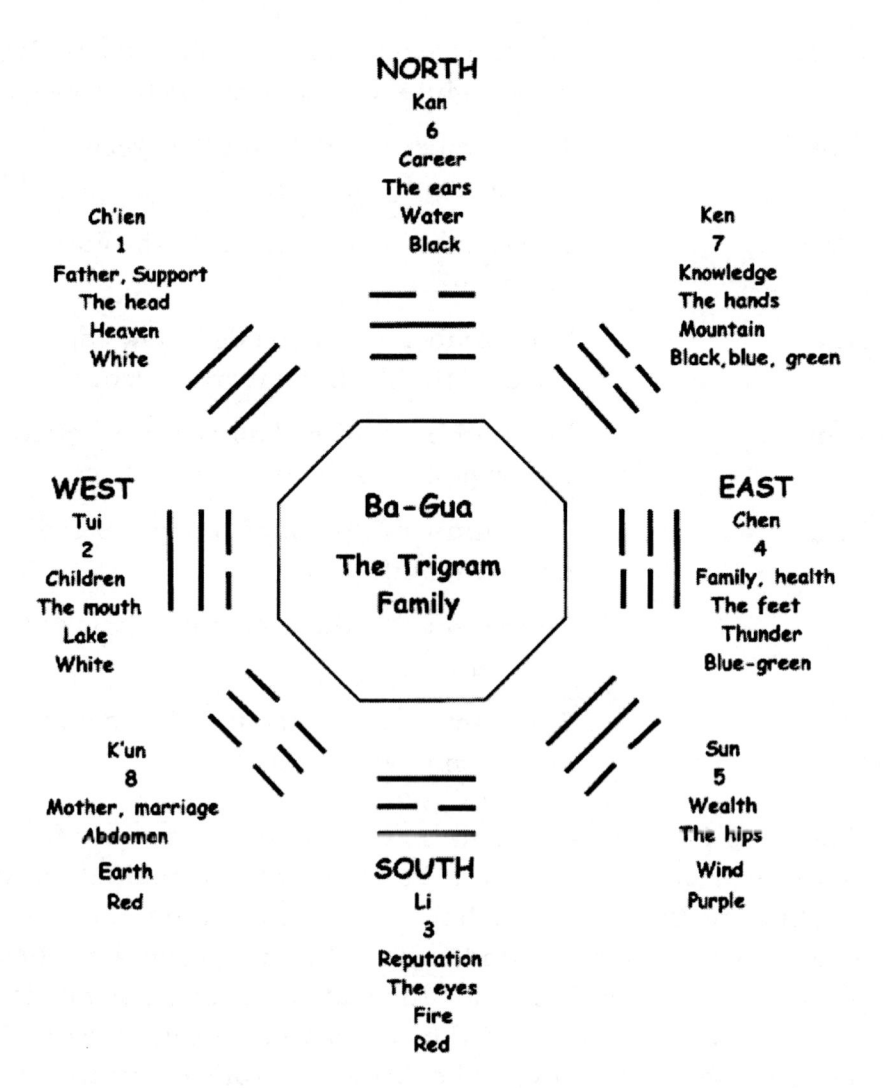

**EAST**
Chen
4
Family, health
The feet
Thunder
Blue-green

**K'un**
8
Mother, marriage
Abdomen
Earth
Red

**Sun**
5
Wealth
The hips
Wind
Purple

**SOUTH**
Li
3
Reputation
The eyes
Fire
Red

*Note that in this diagram the lines are read from outside towards the middle.*

Other attributes associated with the trigrams for the purpose of divination are:

**Ch'ien** — The number 1, the head of the body, the colour white, people arriving in support.

**Chen** — The number 4, the feet, blue-green colour, family and health.

**K'an** — The number 6, colour black, the ears, one's career.

**Ken** — The number 7, the hands, knowledge, the colours black, blue and green.

**K'un** — The number 8, the abdomen, the colours red or pink, marriage.

**Sun** — The number 5, the hips, purple or red colour, wealth.

**Li** — The number 3, the eyes, the colour red, fame or status.

**Tui** — The number 2, the mouth, the colour white, children.

When the I Ching is consulted, one obtains a six-line figure called a hexagram. This is to be seen as the combination, or meeting, of two trigrams: lines 1, 2 and 3 form the Lower Trigram while lines 4, 5 and 6 form the Upper Trigram. These are to be considered first, for their attributes and symbolism will yield a description of the underlying forces at work in one's situation. Moreover, the Lower Trigram represents the inner world of the mind, what is hidden or emerging, while the Upper Trigram represents the outer or material world where events are happening.

Some diviners will take this analysis one step further. If we consider lines 2, 3 and 4 as forming an 'inner lower trigram', while lines 3, 4 and 5 form an 'inner upper trigram', then putting these together yields a new, so-called Nuclear Hexagram. This is thought to describe the hidden energies or possibilities at the heart of one's question.

Φ

There is more about these observations in 'How to do a reading' later. But here is one example that demonstrates the meaningfulness of the trigrams.

Ms W and her partner Mr Y had lived together happily for several years but their relationship was now strained. On the face of it, it seemed that Mr Y had become less committed but there was no obvious reason or particular issue. Ms W consulted the I Ching and asked the question: "What is the future for our relationship?"

This is Hexagram 59, called Dispersion. We notice that the upper trigram is Sun, the eldest daughter, while the lower trigram is K'an, the second son. Sun's gentle wind is blowing over K'an's rushing water. At first sight, the name of the hexagram might suggest 'separation' but this is not the case; rather, Sun penetrates to the cause of the trouble and calms it down. The trouble is in the world of the mind (specifically, Mr Y's mind!) while in the real world Sun suggests how to deal with it. In this particular case, one might even say that the *man's* energy is being cared for by the *woman's* actions.

In the Book, the 'Judgement' for this hexagram speaks of "Success. The king approaches his temple. It furthers one to cross the great water. Perseverance furthers."

Success is suggested because "divisive egotism" is being dissolved. In our context, this means that one or both partners have in their own ways (and no doubt for good reasons to do with life's circumstances) been rather too focused on their own interests and needs. Self-interest is a very natural reaction to difficult challenges in life, but of course it can create a distance between partners. However, the hexagram suggests that it is perfectly possible to overcome this state of affairs (*if those involved choose to*); the energies of the two trigrams are meeting, not moving apart. This means that the partners can work together. (The text is indeed very similar to that of another hexagram called Gathering Together, in which those who have been separated are reunited.)

"The king approaches his temple" also means that everything is in its proper place here, and whoever is the 'leader' in this situation has the power to bring people together. "It furthers one to cross the great water" means that Ms W and Mr Y have the ability to achieve great things and to succeed in difficult undertakings, given that "Perseverance furthers" - determination and integrity are needed. One must be free of personal and separatist motives.

So the answer to the question is that these two people have an essentially strong bond and now face the 'simple' choice of whether or not they wish to do the personal work necessary for the good health of their relationship.

Incidentally, the Nuclear Hexagram (formed from inner trigrams) in this case is Hexagram 27, called Nourishment. What we need to nourish us takes many forms, from food to pleasure, from love to security to spiritual growth. The central and deep issue for the relationship in question was Mr Y's sense of insecurity and his dissatisfaction with aspects of his life.

## Summary

- At the heart of an I Ching reading are groups of three lines called trigrams, made up of unbroken and broken lines.
- There are eight trigrams, each with its own name, attributes and image and other associated qualities.
- It is the combination of these attributes that produces the description of the real forces at work in one's situation, so any reading (of a hexagram) must first consider the component trigrams.
- The yang trigrams are Ch'ien, Chen, K'an and Ken (the 'father', then the eldest, middle and youngest 'sons' of the trigram family). They show how creativity and power are expressed in the world, moving through successive stages.
- The yin trigrams are K'un, Sun, Li and Tui (the 'mother' and three 'daughters' of the family), who express the unfolding effects of perseverance and gentleness in human life.
- The lower trigram of a reading represents forces in the world of the mind, usually hidden from view but which will emerge.
- The upper trigram of a reading shows events occurring in the real world.
- A hexagram also contains within it 'inner trigrams' that can be put together to form a 'nuclear hexagram' describing deep issues at the heart of a situation.

# Forming Your Question

Communication has never truly taken place unless the 'receiver' has clearly understood what the 'sender' has said *and* what their intentions were in saying it.

Suppose you are in a foreign country and needed to ask a local man who doesn't speak English for some directions. You will need to know something of his *language*, both for phrasing the question and for understanding the answer. *Clarity* is going to be essential in both respects. You will also need to feel confident that he really does know the area; in turn he might need to know, in order to give you the best advice, other information such as what type of vehicle you're in, who is travelling with you, how much fuel you have, and whether you're in a hurry or would like to explore the area...The situation is fraught with difficulty and indeed it may be best that you use a handy trusted interpreter.

So it is when addressing the unconscious mind using the I Ching. Our inner mind does not use the same kind of language that we do in normal waking life: it is symbolic, metaphorical and abstract, and the narrative does not always follow linear time (think of how dreams express themselves). The Book is our interpreter because it is deliberately written in just that form, as an intermediary between our language and that of the mind. This is also why, of course, we sometimes find it hard to understand completely its responses. [This is also why we should, I suggest, be wary of 'modern and straightforward' translations, for while perhaps they may be more immediately comprehensible they can miss or gloss over the subtle spirit of the words.]

Equally, when we address the Book with a question, it is clear that we should first give the matter some careful thought. After all, we have arrived at this point as a result of some kind of unrest or anxiety, perhaps a sense that there are unknown forces at work that we need to know more about. It would be wise, therefore, to take some time and examine all the issues around and relating to the question, asking ourselves how we feel about these things and whether there are particular fears or memories associated with them.

For example, suppose you are in an intimate relationship and intend to ask a question such as "Will this relationship be successful?" It would be wise to pause at this point and ask *yourself* further questions such as "Why do I want to ask this question now?" and "Am I having doubts because of past experiences with other people?" and "Is there something about my partner that gives me a problem?" and "Do I have difficulty trusting people?" and "What does it mean for a relationship to be 'successful' anyway?" It is not always necessary actually to *answer* all such questions! But on the one hand this self-examination helps the unconscious mind to focus on the real issues at stake, and on the other hand it may help you to realise that the question you intended to ask may not be the really fundamental one facing you after all.

Having accepted, then, that our own thoughts and intentions need to be clear, we must also take into consideration the way that the Book can talk back to us. One would not choose randomly a five-year old French child and ask them to explain nuclear physics in Urdu. Our questions must be appropriate to the form of language and the kind of advice that the I Ching is written to offer. Such advice is personal, and ethical, and predicated on what is best for the general course of our lives as human and spiritual beings. One does not ask "Will I win the lottery this week?", not just because it is not the fundamental question (which is about fear of financial insecurity), nor even because it is somehow superficial (financial security is important), but because the I Ching is not written in those terms. For one thing, in the world of the spirit, a period of time such as one week is entirely irrelevant. For another thing, a lottery is merely one way among many others (and an utterly random one at that) of providing what we are really seeking, so by expressing the question in this way we are putting *conditions* and *restrictions* on the kind of answer we can receive. We must allow the Book (that is, our inner mind) to respond to us in the way it needs to, by addressing what is actually important and necessary for our life, so we must leave the question more 'open'. [9]

There will be times, of course, when we're not even quite sure what the question is. We feel somehow uneasy or vaguely dissatisfied, perhaps our lives seem to lack direction, or we know that there is 'something in the air' but can't put a finger on it. As it happens, this doesn't matter at all and it is perfectly acceptable to go ahead with a reading provided that we have first done some self-examination as described above. The point is that while our conscious minds may not know what the issue is, our deeper minds *do* know it, and that is why we felt the impulse to do a consultation in the first place. So we can approach the I Ching with open heart and open mind, and ask for guidance without forming any specific question at all.

---

[9] If one did in fact ask such a question, the Book has a way of dealing with it. It will either, reasonably politely, tell one to go away and think again or, if it is feeling charitable, it might actually answer the true underlying question. In the latter case, of course, one might find it difficult to understand the response if one hasn't first examined for oneself what that underlying question is.

## Examples of bad or inappropriate questions

"When will I meet my soulmate?"
"Will I get a good job this year?"
"C seems like a nice man – should I have sex with him?"
"How can I get the house of my dreams?"
"I don't trust A – what's wrong with her?"
"Am I going to win enough money to pay off my credit card?"
"B isn't working well – shall I sack him?"
"I didn't understand the last answer – will you tell me again?"

## Examples of better, more appropriate questions

"Will I find happiness with a loving partner?"
"What kind of work would really suit me?"
"Will C and I be happy together?"
"What do I need to make me feel secure?"
"How can I deal with my feelings of distrust towards A?"
"What can I do to feel more secure financially?"
"Why isn't B working well?"
" ? "

Even if we have given careful thought to our question and phrased it well, there may be times when we genuinely don't understand the Book's answer. So is it acceptable to ask again? And can we ask any number of perhaps supplementary questions?

The first thing to say is that, yes, it is quite possible for something to have 'gone wrong' with the consultation. Perhaps we weren't really in the right state of mind, or there was some disturbance during the procedure; maybe we hurried it or wrote the hexagram down incorrectly. If there is genuinely a mismatch between question and answer then the fault will lie with us and our conscious world, not with the Book. The Book is by its very nature an innocent party. Moreover, our Higher Self that knows us perfectly and loves us unconditionally will not mislead us. So the best thing to do in these circumstances is to ignore the reading, and go away to clear the head before trying again later.

However, perhaps we should ask ourselves instead whether the misunderstanding is in fact due to the response *not being what we expected*, or (and this is frequently the case) due to it being the perfect response to *a different question* – the real and more immediate one that's in our mind. Suppose you are worried both about finances and the relationship with your partner, because you just had an argument about money. Out of loyalty to the other, your question may have been about finances; whereas what is really causing turmoil in your mind is your emotional security. We can always trust the deeper mind to know what is most important for us.

For these reasons, it is almost never appropriate to repeat one's question (unless one is quite sure that something has gone wrong). Instead, it would be wise to allow some time to pass while thinking over the response carefully, so that it may permeate, or reform itself in, our thoughts. Then, if it still doesn't make sense, one might consult the Book again with a slightly different question (and, perhaps, an apology to one's inner self). How soon and how often? This will always be a matter of personal judgement, but given all that has been said so far it is evident that we should approach the process both peacefully and mindfully – achieving clarity and the right circumstances can take some time. For myself, I always allow at least one day and night; there is no hurry on the spiritual path.

Ф

All of these considerations have implied adopting a certain state of mind when approaching the I Ching. To recognise that state, let us consider the 'spirit' of the Book itself.

We do not quite know, of course, what is really going on when we consult the I Ching. How is it, anyway, that despite being an ancient Chinese invention, it works just as well in modern times and for all human conditions, not just Chinese ones? It is clearly touching something deep in the human mind that is universal; its symbolism and imagery are archetypal. For example, the commentaries in the Book often refer to what 'the superior man' should do in a certain situation. Originally, this meant a Chinese aristocrat since these were the people who made pretty much all the decisions for everyone else. But we can also now understand the phrase to mean anyone who is sincerely trying to understand the laws of nature and wisely adapt his or her own behaviour to them. The descriptions of situations and of right actions that we read in the Book's pages resonate with abstract concepts in our unconscious mind (Carl Jung would say our 'collective unconscious'). Sometimes we can intuitively see these below the surface of an event – an argument at work, say, is really a power struggle due to psychological insecurity – and sometimes we need to go deeper than that, or access wider information that we don't know consciously.

Confucius taught that every event in the real world is the effect of an image, or an idea, in the unseen world. Mankind is unique in that our consciousness links us with both Heaven (the world of ideas) and Earth (the physical world of visible things). It is down to the sages or holy men, he said, to contact that higher world through their intuition and so help other people to intervene in worldly events. Wilhelm wrote that the I Ching is thus a tool for helping us to discern "the seeds of things to come". Now, this language is not very different to our modern way of speaking about 'energies' –

forces at work under the surface of our lives and bringing about situations in our real world later. But these forces or energies are not physical, so we have to reach into a higher level of consciousness to perceive them. This is very similar to what seems to happen in our dream world, where the Higher Self can sometimes bring to our awareness information and guidance that we are not conscious of in everyday life. Somehow the I Ching, because its symbolism embodies the true spirit of human life, enables us to connect with that higher consciousness when we are awake.

In the language of Confucius, we are "reaching into Heaven" itself. The modern spiritual teacher Deepak Chopra might say we are "touching the Field of Pure Potential". This is why every serious student of the I Ching will say that the Book should be treated with a certain reverence. "It requires a clear and tranquil mind", said Wilhelm [10], and Carl Jung went further, saying "It is not for the frivolous or the immature."

To consult the I Ching is a spiritual act. This is so just as much when our question is about money as when it is about love or service to others. [11] Now, there are as many ways to think about spirituality as there people on the planet, and everyone should adopt an approach that feels right for them; the Book contains no dogma, doctrine or creed save that our attitude be one of an honest heart and a genuine willingness to be guided. After all, the suggestion that we are actually addressing our inner selves is a difficult concept. There are those who may wish to 'ritualise' the consultation in some way, using prayer or candles or physical self-cleansing. Others will meditate for a while and then launch into it. Some will personify the Book itself (as the ancient Chinese did) by

---

10 He might have added, though it should be obvious, "...and a tranquil room with the `phone turned off."
11 Incidentally, because the entire purpose of the Book is to support the spiritual path, it will very quickly be discovered that it just cannot be used with any ill-intention, or manipulatively, or with any selfish hidden agenda.

addressing the spirit within it [12] or by imagining it to speak with the voice of a wise old friend or teacher. None of these approaches matters at all as long as they are carried out with *respect*. The counsel of the I Ching is not a matter of personal belief.

Given all the considerations discussed here, about preparing oneself, one's environment and one's question, anyone can use the I Ching confidently.

Quite *why* this is so, it must be said, is still something of a mystery. But throughout history there have been many relatively successful methods of divination and they have certain common factors. Firstly, there is someone who poses the question, usually a seer or shaman of some kind who has special skills and acts on behalf of the enquirer; the latter must also be present or somehow personally involved in the process because the issue at stake is within their mind (if not also the answer to that issue). Secondly there is a form of symbolic language or imagery (such as Tarot cards or runes or star patterns or tea leaves) by means of which an answer can be perceived. The source of the answer has usually been attributed to 'spirits' of some kind. In the case of the I Ching, the seer can be you yourself, while the Book is the symbolic form. You are also the source of the answer.

The third and really intriguing factor is what links the other two together meaningfully: a *random* act such as choosing cards or tossing coins. Since we cannot answer our question in a rational way (or we wouldn't need to ask it), we need a non-rational method that is beyond our conscious control or influence. It is a physical act in this conscious world (Earth) that is appropriate to the symbolic language we are using, which in turn embodies the information and meanings of the hidden unconscious world (Heaven). If we believe that it is the energy of the inner mind that is *causing* the fall of the cards

---

12 Note that this is different to "the spirit of it".

or coins, then what is happening is psychokinesis. However we think of this, the essential point is that we are not deliberately involved in the process. So this is why, again, the question must be considered and phrased carefully, and the procedure approached with some reverence.

Carl Jung believed that the consultation process was a prime example of his theory of synchronicity i.e. a coincidence that has genuine meaningfulness for the person involved. The coincidence here is the chance result of the method used with the mental state of the person doing it *at that moment in time*. Here is another reason, then, for not questioning the Book repetitively or too frequently. It is also the reason why using an Internet site to get an I Ching reading is entirely pointless! Not only is it not a very respectful method, but more importantly one's inner mind cannot properly be engaged with the process.

## Summary

- We should consider carefully all the issues relating to our question.
- We should phrase the question openly and without pre-conditions.
- If something goes wrong with the procedure, we should ignore the result and let some time pass before trying again.
- If we don't understand an answer, it should not be rejected – it may have a deeper meaning for us or it may be the answer to a more important question.
- The same question should not be repeated.
- We should not use the Book too frequently.
- The I Ching describes the forces at work beneath the surface of life, connecting us to our higher consciousness.
- A consultation is a spiritual act and should be approached with some reverence.
- The method used must be genuinely random and beyond our conscious influence or control.

# Methods for Consulting the I Ching

The I Ching is a wonderful book that can give us genuinely wise and useful advice on all sorts of problems, from the practical and down-to-earth to the moral and the spiritual. But naturally, this can only happen if we give careful thought to the question posed and carry out the consultation in a proper manner.

This chapter describes several different methods of consulting the I Ching, each of which has advantages and disadvantages. It is suggested that you try out a few of them to discover which one feels right for you. Apart from the obvious differences in actually carrying them out, they do not all work in the same way: the various possible outcomes do not always have the same probability. The reasons for this are given in Appendix A and you must decide for yourself how important those considerations are.

According to ancient tradition, the common method of consultation was to use of a bundle of yarrow stalks; then around a thousand years ago the use of Chinese coins became more popular. These items are available from specialist suppliers, but it is quite acceptable to substitute any wooden sticks or modern coins. Whatever objects are used, they should really be new and kept specifically for this sole purpose so that their 'energy' is not tainted by external influences. As described in the last chapter, these objects are personal and special for you, used in a spiritual act of creating a synchronicity between your deepest mind (the world of Heaven) and your conscious concerns (in the material world of Earth).

Most of the following methods adopt the same conventions:

1  An action is performed (such as tossing a coin) which results in either a 'yang' or a 'yin' outcome.
2  Yang is given the numerical value 3, and yin is given the value 2. [13]
3  The action is performed three times and the numerical values are added.
4  The result is either 6 or 7 or 8 or 9, each of which describes a particular type of line in a 'hexagram'.
5  The first time this is done one creates the first and lowest line of the hexagram, and the process is then repeated five more times, developing the six-line figure (or two trigrams) from the bottom upwards.
6  The four types of outcome, or line, are as follows:

yin + yin + yin = 2 + 2 + 2 = 6 ...... a 'moving yin line'

—— x ——

yin + yin + yang = 2 + 2 + 3 = 7 ...... a 'yang line'

─────────

---

13 It is unclear why the simpler values 1 and 2 were not given, except perhaps that odd numbers were regarded as 'strong' because they have a 'centre', thus 3 is the first true odd number.

# LIGHTING THE PATH

yin + yang + yang = 2 + 3 + 3 = 8 ...... a 'yin line'

—— ——

yang + yang + yang = 3 + 3 + 3 = 9 ...... a 'moving yang line'

——o——

(The *order* of the 2s and 3s doesn't matter here.)

The reasoning behind this is as follows. Yin and yang are the two essential principles that represent the duality of human experience, and *both* of them are needed in some kind of balance for life to be meaningful. With the outcome '7' the yang is said to be balanced, or held in check, by the two yins, so the quality of the line is yang. Similarly, the quality of the '8' line is yin. But when all three results have the same value (such as yin + yin + yin) there is an imbalance; so while such a line has an obvious yin or yang quality it cannot stay like that and must be 'moving'. These lines indicate specific changes in a situation.

## The Yarrow Stalks Method

**Step 1**      Take 50 stalks and discard one (this is 'the observer'), leaving 49. Divide these randomly into left (L) and right (R) piles.

**Step 2**      Take 1 from R: this is the first part of the Step 2 result. Now take groups of 4 from L until there is a remainder of 1, 2, 3 or 4: this remainder is the second part of the Step 2 result. Now take groups of 4 from R until there is a remainder of 1, 2, 3 or 4: this remainder is the third part of the Step 2 result. The remainders result in either (1,4,0) which is ignored (start again), or (1,1,3) or (1,2,2) or (1,3,1) which count as yang with value **3**, or (1,4,4) which counts as yin with value **2**. Discard these 5 or 9 stalks; gather the other stalks together and redivide them.

**Step 3**      Repeat Step 2 (i.e. take 1 from R, then 4s from L, then 4s from R). The remainders result in either (1,3,0) which is ignored (start again), or (1,1,2) or (1,2,1) which count as yang with value **3**, or (1,3,4) or (1,4,3) which count as yin with value **2**. Discard these 4 or 8 stalks; gather the other stalks together and redivide them.

**Step 4**      Repeat Step 2 again. The results now are the same as for Step 3.

| | |
|---|---|
| **Step 5** | Add together the results from Steps 2, 3 and 4 to get **6**, **7**, **8** or **9**. These represent, respectively, a moving yin line, a yang line, a yin line or a moving yang line – the first (lowest) line of the hexagram. |
| **Step 6** | Repeat the entire procedure from Step 1 five more times! |

This is a time-consuming (15 – 20 minutes) and tricky method that engages one's mind fully. Its benefit is said to be that the meditative form allows the unconscious to become immersed fully in the problem posed. On the other hand, unless one is completely familiar and at ease with the method, one's concentration and perhaps anxiety might interfere with this.

Another possible problem with the yarrow stalks is that while the actions taken are indeed random (a prerequisite for synchronicity to occur), the method is not mathematically 'fair'. That is, the likelihood of the outcome being 'yang' is not equal to that of 'yin'. [14] There are those who argue that not only is this irrelevant (since the unconscious mind will take account of it), it is also actually *natural* since yang has a tendency to action and movement while yin is yielding and passive...

## The Marbles Method

This is a modern invention that replicates the probabilities of the Yarrow Stalks method (for those who adhere to that way of thinking) but is far simpler to carry out. Some might argue that it is *too* quick and simple.

Obtain a number of marbles of the same size in four different colours (one may use anything similar, such as coloured

---

[14] See Appendix A for the mathematics associated with all these methods.

discs of the same shape and size). Let one colour represent 'yin', a different colour for 'yang', a third colour for 'moving yin' and the fourth for 'moving yang'. Remember which is which!

How many marbles or discs are required? In order to replicate the Yarrow Stalks method exactly there should be 17 for yin, 11 for yang, 2 for moving yin and 8 for moving yang. So 38 marbles or discs are needed. A simpler though slightly less accurate division is 9 for yin, 6 for yang, 1 for moving yin and 4 for moving yang (a total of 20 marbles or discs).

Put the marbles or discs into a bowl or linen bag, mix them up, then focus on the question and choose just *one* without looking and note its colour. This is the first line of your hexagram. Replace the marble or disc and repeat the process another five times.

## The Coins Method

Three coins of the same type are used, where one face (usually 'tails') is designated 'yin' with a numerical value **2** and the other face ('heads') is designated 'yang' with value **3**. Many people like to use Chinese coins, but this is not important in itself; however, whatever type is used they should be new and used solely for this purpose. The coins are tossed within the palms for a few moments and then thrown down, their face values added.

The results will be **6**, **7**, **8** or **9** which represent, respectively, a moving yin line, a yang line, a yin line and a moving yang line. This is the first (lowest) line of the hexagram. The procedure is then repeated five times.

This is the method most widely adopted in the present day. In contrast to the previous methods, the probabilities of yin and yang (and of moving yin and moving yang) are equal here so the method is 'fair'. But because it is easy and quick, it is all the more important that the observer should carefully adopt the right state of mind (calm, quiet, reverent) and focus closely on the question at hand.

## The Playing Cards Method

Take a standard pack of playing cards (without jokers), where red cards (diamonds and hearts) are designated 'yin' with numerical value **2** and black cards (clubs and spades) are designated 'yang' with value **3**. The pack is thoroughly shuffled while one focuses on the question and then three cards are chosen at random; when one is chosen *it is not replaced* before the next choice.

The numerical values are added, resulting in **6**, **7**, **8** or **9** which represent, respectively, a moving yin line, a yang line, a yin line and a moving yang line. This is the first (lowest) line of the hexagram. The chosen cards are replaced in the pack and the procedure is then repeated another five times.

The frequent shuffling of the cards means that the method can be quite meditative, and it is not as 'quick and easy' as the Coins method. However, some might feel that it is not really 'appropriate' given the cards' association with games and gambling! This problem is overcome by the following methods.

## Personalised Methods

It is quite possible to devise for oneself alternative personal methods of consulting the Book, which has the advantage of encouraging a closer and deeper connection to one's own unconscious mind. Clearly, this should not be done casually;

the method should have a feeling of reverence and be dedicated to this sole purpose.

This first example replicates the Playing Cards method. Make a number of Personal Cards that are easy to handle (say, 8 x 5 cm) and are identical in appearance on the reverse side. On the faces of the cards draw a number **2** for yin or a number **3** for yang; instead, one could draw any pleasing symbols or images that will represent these principles (something 'earthy' or 'shadowy' to represent yin, something 'heavenly' or 'light' to represent yang). One then chooses three cards from the pack while focusing on the question; when one card is chosen it is not replaced before the next choice. Add the numerical values of the cards chosen to form the first (lowest) line of the hexagram, then replace the cards, shuffle and repeat the procedure another five times.

The numerical totals will be either **6**, **7**, **8** or **9** which represent, respectively, a moving yin line, a yang line, a yin line and a moving yang line.

How many of each card are needed? Clearly, the minimum number is three of each, thus six in total. However, mathematics shows that at least forty-six cards (twenty-three of each type) are required in order to replicate the sort of results obtained by the more traditional methods!

A second example of a personalised method is one that I shall call Short Cut Cards. Instead of using cards that represent yin (2) or yang (3), and then choosing three of them to make up a line, one could make cards that themselves show all four possible lines: yin, yang, moving yin and moving yang. Then choosing just *one card* (instead of three) gives the result for each line of the hexagram.

Make a set of cards again, say, 8 x 5 cm and identical in appearance on the reverse side. On the faces, draw the numbers 6, 7, 8 or 9 to represent moving yin, yang, yin and moving yang lines respectively. Alternatively, draw the symbols for these lines as shown at the beginning of this chapter, or four different and clearly identifiable images to represent them.

The cards are shuffled while focusing on the question and then just one is chosen; this gives the first (lowest) line of the hexagram. The card is then replaced, the pack shuffled, and the procedure repeated another five times.

How many of each card are needed? The more traditional methods of consultation yield an average of about 1.5 moving lines per hexagram (which means 4.5 non-moving lines). So if we want to replicate this, the ratio of moving lines to non-moving lines has to be 1 : 3. But of course the numbers must be even so that one can have an equal number of each type of card to choose from. So the minimum number of cards required is eight: one each of moving yin and moving yang cards, and three each of yin and yang cards. This method effectively replicates the probabilities of the Coins method, which also has eight possible outcomes for each line of the hexagram.

A final suggestion combines the last method with an earlier one, in the interests of variety. Instead of using cards one could use eight marbles or discs (or any interesting, appropriate and identical objects!) in four colours. We need one marble to represent a moving yin line, one marble of a different colour to represent a moving yang line, three marbles of a third colour for a yin line and three of a fourth colour to represent a yang line. (Appropriate colours might be pink, grey, red and black.)

Making one's own personal and perhaps decorated cards or other objects brings a closer connection to the Book. However, the method for using them should not be *so simple and quick* that some of the meditative aspect of the consultation is lost.

## Summary

- Whichever method is used for a consultation, one's preparation must be careful and the method carried out mindfully.
- According to tradition, yin has the numerical value 2 and yang has the value 3.
- When three of these are combined the outcome is either 6, 7, 8 or 9.
- 6 represents a 'moving yin line'; 7 represents a 'yang line'; 8 represents a 'yin line'; 9 represents a 'moving yang line'.
- The most traditional method is to use 50 yarrow stalks. This is meditative but time-consuming, and the probabilities of each type of outcome are not equal.
- A method that replicates the yarrow stalk probabilities but is much easier to carry out is to use 38 coloured marbles or discs.
- The most popular method is to use three coins; this is simple and fairly quick.
- Using a pack of playing cards is also simple but has the advantage of being more meditative.
- Devising one's own personal method can bring a deeper connection to the I Ching, as long as care is taken to make sure that it yields the right kind of results. One can use cards, marbles, discs or any other similar decorated or coloured objects.

# How to Do a Reading

Before beginning a consultation of the I Ching there are three things that must be considered carefully.

The most essential of these is to decide on one's question and how to phrase it. This seems obvious perhaps, but we should remember that a good reading connects us with our deepest mind where everything that is really important to us is known and understood. Therefore, for example, if the question that we ask is not *the real question* that is actually troubling us then we are unlikely to recognise the response that the Book gives. Again, if we ask our question in a frivolous or repetitive way, we are likely to receive Hexagram 4 in reply: this basically says "Go away and stop bothering me."

When I was first learning about computers, I wrote a program that would generate an I Ching hexagram randomly. The first time that I used it, I received Hexagram 4! This was, I'm sure, because my motives and preparation were not genuine and my inner consciousness not properly engaged in the process.

The second point, as just suggested, is that our state of mind must be right and our circumstances prepared so that we are fully engaged without any distraction. The actual reading will take 10 – 20 minutes (not counting the interpretation of it) and we should not be hurried or disturbed during this. A consultation of the I Ching is not a religious act but it is a spiritual one, and we should approach it with due reverence. (The interpretation of the result might sometimes be easy, but equally it can take several hours of careful thought!)

So, on both the above points, please read the chapter 'Forming your question' before beginning a reading.

Finally, we need to be completely conversant with the *method* we are going to use (see the last chapter), so that our reading is not interrupted by any uncertainty about how to carry it out. It is a good idea to choose the method that appeals and then practise it first without asking a question. Do the same thing if you have used the Book before but intend to try a new method of consultation. Even so, it is possible for something to 'go wrong' during a reading: a coin might be dropped on the floor, or we forget to gather up and redivide the yarrow stalks, or our child might walk into the room... In such situations we should stop the reading, collect our thoughts and compose our mind, then start again. After all, this question is important for us!

Ф

Let's do a reading. I'll go through one step by step here. But you might like to do your own practice reading alongside this.

I have prepared my room, lit a candle and some incense to help me focus calmly, and spent a few moments in quiet meditation asking 'the spirit' for guidance.

On a fresh piece of paper, I write the date and my question:

> "Should I accept the business opportunity I have just received?" [15]

---

15 This is a true reading. I have just received such an offer.

## LIGHTING THE PATH

I have been going through some frustrating times lately in the development of my literary work, but a friend has suggested an opportunity to me. The idea is attractive but it will involve hard work and I shall need others' help. I am using the Coins method, with three Chinese coins that I keep for this purpose.

- I focus on my question, toss the coins within my palms for about half a minute, and then throw them gently onto the table in front of me. The result is three heads with numerical value 9, signifying a moving yang line. I make a note on the paper of the result, as shown at the beginning of the last chapter. This is the first and lowest line of my hexagram.
- I repeat the process, resulting in two heads and a tail which have value 8, a yin line, and record it.
- The next line is yang, resulting from two tails and a head, with value 7.
- The fourth line is the same as the second one.
- The fifth line is a moving yin, from three tails, with value 6.
- The top and last line is yang, the same as the third line.

The results of my reading have been recorded thus:

```
7  ──────────
6  ───  X  ───
8  ───     ───
7  ──────────
8  ───     ───
9  ───  O  ───
```

## Step One: Identify the trigrams

Ignoring for the moment whether lines are 'moving' or not, we see that the lower trigram is Li, the second daughter of the trigram family whose attributes are the illumination and warmth of fire, and the bringing of nourishment. The lower trigram represents the 'inner world' of the mind in this situation, so Li is very appropriate: through my writing I am trying to develop understanding, for myself and others, of the human condition – and gain an income! The upper trigram represents the situation in the real 'outer world'. Here it is Ken, the youngest son who brings activities in the world to completion and clarifies what has been achieved: this is indeed what I am hoping for through the opportunity that has been offered to me.

## Step Two (optional): Identify the nuclear hexagram

If the initial response in Step One is at all unclear, or we feel that there might be a deeper underlying impulse for our question, it can sometimes be helpful to consider the 'hidden' or inner hexagram of our result. We do not need to do this if we already know that our reading is on the right track.

The nuclear hexagram is formed by identifying two new 'inner trigrams' within our result: the lower inner trigram is formed by the second, third and fourth lines, and the upper inner trigram is formed by the third, fourth and fifth lines. Again, the movement of lines is ignored for the moment so my fifth line, above, is simply regarded as yin.

My nuclear hexagram is thus:

```
── ──
── ──
───────
── ──
───────
── ──
```

The upper trigram is Chen and the lower trigram is K'an. We now check the hexagram key given in the I Ching book (in Wilhelm's edition it is at the back). With Chen as the upper trigram and K'an as the lower, we find that the number of the hexagram they form is 40, whose name is Deliverance.

Turning to this chapter in the Book, we read the text of this hexagram describing a time when difficulties begin to be eased and tensions resolved, clearing the air – exactly what my inner mind is hoping for by considering this question.

## Step Three: Identify the answer hexagram

Still ignoring lines' movement, we now check again the hexagram key given in the I Ching book. With Li as the upper trigram and Ken as the lower, we find that the number of the hexagram they form is 22, whose name is Grace. This is the first part of the answer to my question.

Turning to chapter 22, we read a 'Judgement' or Commentary that describes my situation in general terms. "Success in small matters. It is favourable to undertake something." This at first seems to suggest that the action I am contemplating is 'a good thing' but not likely to yield great achievements. To be honest, the original accompanying text for this particular hexagram is quite difficult to interpret; usually, it describes a situation of clarity and peace, but one that may be too brief to resolve very serious matters. Yet it does speak of strong traditions (here, literature) made "pleasing by beauty" in the human world and having some influence (which is what I hope for). The essential point for me, though, is that this hexagram relates to spiritual matters and to the world of the arts; in these respects, it is entirely appropriate to my situation and to my question.

## Step Four: Consider the moving lines

As the name of the Book suggests, there is movement and change implicit in every part of a situation, so the lines of a hexagram are to be understood as representing stages of this potential movement:

| | |
|---|---|
| **6th line** | Passing the peak of change |
| **5th line** | The peak of a situation |
| **4th line** | Approaching the full potential |
| **3rd line** | Expansion of the situation |
| **2nd line** | The beginning |
| **1st line** | What is about to come |

Note that the movement is always to be considered from the lowest line upwards. And if any of the lines in our original reading are moving ones, then these are drawing our attention to specific information or advice about the situation, and we should read, in order, the commentaries associated with them.

Of course, it is possible that we have no moving lines. This does not mean that the situation in question will never change – the whole philosophy of the Book is that things are always moving and developing – but that we have the substance of our answer already provided. If we need more information than this, it would be perfectly appropriate to ask a supplementary question.

Turning back to the practice reading, the first line was moving (yang) so it indicates something I should be aware of right at the outset concerning the opportunity I'm considering. The original comments written by Wu for the lines are often figurative and poetic, and it is not always easy to see where they've come from, so therefore we concentrate on their interpretations given by later authors.[16] Here, the text refers to "A beginner in a subordinate place" – yes, that's certainly me in my situation, knowing very little about the running of the business. The advice given is that one could look to others to do the work (riding in "a carriage") but that it is better and more proper to accept personal responsibility. So the initial answer to my question is that it would be a good thing to do.

The fifth (yin) line of my reading was also moving, referring to a time when the offer has been accepted and the business is developing. This line describes one who withdraws from people who are interested in luxury; I take this to mean that I should not go into the business with materialistic ambitions, and indeed it is not likely to be very rewarding financially ("the roll of silk is meagre"). However, the text goes on to answer another of my basic concerns, the need for others'

---

[16] On the other hand, it is often surprising and delightful to find that, despite their ancient origins, the actual words can sometimes be directly relevant to us. For example, "cross the great water" usually means that some difficult enterprise or course of action can successfully be undertaken; but it is very likely to crop up when our situation indeed involves a journey abroad. Again, "the south-west furthers" encourages us to get involved with others in some activity or other, but the actual compass direction might itself be meaningful for us. At the end of this book is a glossary of such common words and phrases in the I Ching, but we should always be alert to the possibility of direct meanings. Our inner minds sometimes know something very specific in our interests!

support: "He finds an individual to look up to" and all will go well as long as my motives are sincere.

Notice that the reading is *not* telling me what to do. One always has free will and the ability to choose whether or not to pursue a particular course. My reading has told me that the business is a good thing and that I will get the help I need, but it is unlikely to be very profitable; so if my real interest or need were to make money, then at this point I might choose to turn down the offer.

Before moving on to the last step of the consultation, it is worth adding a couple of other remarks about moving lines. I have described their actual position within the hexagram as meaningful and relating to a situation's development, but there will be odd occasions when this is not so. It may happen that a certain line contains information or advice that we really need to know (so it is shown moving) but it doesn't fall in quite 'the right position' in the hexagram. It is the *meaning* of the line, rather than its position, which is of overriding importance. In fact, this could be said to be true of the fifth line in my own reading above; a fifth line normally refers to a time when the situation is fully developed, but my need for support would be earlier than that!

Then there is the possibility, very rare, that a certain moving line doesn't seem relevant to our question, or hasn't a clear meaning for us. Of course, we should first scratch our heads and search for the meaning; it may refer to an aspect of the question that hadn't occurred to us, or it may be giving a piece of information that we shall need to know later. Such lines must not be ignored. But it can also happen that the Book 'wishes' to give us a particular result hexagram (see the next step), because of something important contained within its text, and the only way it can do that from the starting position of our answer hexagram is to 'insert' a certain moving line.

# LIGHTING THE PATH

## Step Five: Identify the result hexagram

The final step in a consultation is to consider the outcomes resulting from any movement or changes in the answer hexagram. If we allow our situation to develop as described in the latter, and accept the advice given, then the I Ching shows us where the situation is likely to lead. (Remember that this is a matter of probability – nothing is ever fated with certainty especially when several other people and their choices might be involved in our question.) The Book does this by now allowing the moving lines to move and change into their opposite character. [17] In my reading, the first line was a moving yang so now I let it change into a yin line; the fifth line was a moving yin so now it changes into a yang line.

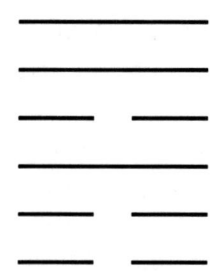

```
———————
———————
———  ———
———————
———  ———
———  ———
```

The upper trigram is now Sun, the gentle penetrating wind of the first daughter of the trigram family (whose other image is wood), while the lower trigram is Ken, the youngest son whom we met earlier in the answer hexagram. It is very appropriate here that the earlier upper trigram has now become the lower one (suggesting forward movement) but in truth we shouldn't expect this to happen very often. Moreover, the earlier description of the trigrams as representing inner and outer worlds is no longer applicable at this stage.

---

[17] A moving line is unstable because it contains only one principle, yin or yang. Therefore at some point it will have to change. A moving yin line, therefore, changes into a yang line and vice-versa.

Turning to the hexagram key in the Book, Sun above with Ken below produces hexagram 53 whose name is Development or Gradual Progress. At this point we read only the main Judgement or Commentary and do not refer to any specific lines. The image of hexagram 53 is of a tree on a mountain, suggesting natural and steady development with secure roots. The text describes a situation in which one moves forward with caution, always maintaining proper relationships with others and taking care to act morally. In this way, it suggests, one can influence other people with "lasting effect". So once again I am being advised that the opportunity I am being offered is likely to be ultimately successful; but once again there is emphasis on the advice that I must proceed carefully and certainly not expect any quick results. (Many hexagrams have alternative interpretations depending of course on the question asked. This one primarily concerns personal relationships, even courtship. The character of the advice is still the same: "be cautious".)

Notice that this result hexagram does not really predict a specific outcome, such as winning a Business Of The Year award or making me rich and famous! But it does answer my underlying concern about security and the development of my work, along with giving further ethical advice about how to achieve them.

To summarise, my interpretation of this consultation is as follows:

> *"This is a good and appropriate business opportunity for you. It will involve some hard work with relatively little financial return. But you will receive the help you need and with the right approach, cautious and ethical, it will achieve influence."*

Φ

## LIGHTING THE PATH

Our hexagrams answer our real concerns and sometimes a result hexagram will contain more straightforward predictions. Suppose my original question had been about the development of my relationship with a girlfriend whom I really care for. Hexagram 22 and its moving lines would then have suggested "This is a beautiful and peaceful relationship; you should work on it and not be worried about having no money" while hexagram 53 could be taken to say "This relationship is secure and you should probably marry her"!

But it has to be said that sometimes a result hexagram does not seem to follow from the answer hexagram (even though the latter were perfectly meaningful). It is as if 'something has gone wrong'. But this cannot be! An I Ching reading simply cannot be inconsistent, because all five steps that I have described are of one single process, a synchronicity of the unconscious and the conscious mind. Moreover, we have sought advice from our own 'Higher Self', who knows us completely, about an issue that is important for us, and that Self cannot be other than trustworthy.

So we can be sure that the result hexagram does hold a meaning for us, even if it takes a while to discover it. As suggested earlier, some hexagrams have secondary meanings depending on the type of question asked. For example, hexagram 38 is Opposition which can clearly have negative implications: there is fire above and water below, they move in opposite directions and of course don't go well together. But the text also refers to the natural polarity of life – Heaven and Earth, light and dark, male and female – which is essential for true creativity.

Again, sometimes, there is *a specific clue* in the wording as to how the changes referred to earlier will come about. In one reading I did for another person, where the answer hexagram was positive, the result hexagram seemed fairly irrelevant until I read the words "recourse to law"! This proved to be indeed what was needed to move that situation on. And we have already seen that in my own practice reading in this chapter, the result hexagram re-emphasised the advice given in the answer hexagram while also answering one of my deeper concerns with the words "secure roots".

Finally, if none of the above remarks seem appropriate yet the answer hexagram doesn't appear to follow, there is the possibility that the Book is giving a stark warning of the consequences if the advice given earlier is NOT heeded. This was, I think, the case with a friend who drew hexagram 12 named Standstill - a powerful statement that the success indicated by the answer hexagram would only come about if he adopted a spiritual rather than a materialistic attitude in approaching his predicament (it was quite a personal challenge!).

As one is developing a relationship with the I Ching, one soon finds that its responses are astonishingly accurate and can be trusted. There will, however, naturally be some readings that are difficult to interpret. But please be reassured that provided you have prepared yourself and your environment well, and carried out the chosen method correctly, the answers you receive will be both meaningful and in your highest interests.

## Summary

- We must give careful thought in advance to the question we are going to ask and how to phrase it; it must be the question that is of greatest importance to us at this time.
- We must ensure that the environment is calm and undisturbed.
- We must be fully conversant with the method that is to be used.
- The mind must be calm and focused on the question throughout the consultation.
- Carry out the method to obtain each of the six lines in turn, starting with the lowest, and record the results.
- Step One: identify the two trigrams, the lower representing the inner world of the mind and the upper representing the outer world, and consider their meanings.
- Step Two: identify the nuclear hexagram, which reveals one's deeper motives and concerns. This is optional.
- Step Three: identify the answer hexagram and read the Judgement and associated Commentary, which describe the situation in general terms.
- Step Four: consider in turn the moving lines and the specific advice or information the text offers. The position of these lines within the hexagram can also be significant.
- Step Five: let the moving lines change in character to produce a result hexagram, which usually describes the likely outcome of following the advice or course of action suggested in the answer.

# Examples of I Ching Readings

You have probably realised by now that actually carrying out an I Ching consultation is a relatively easy process; the tricky part can be the interpretation of the result!

Several hexagrams have different levels of meaning, just as our own minds work on many levels of consciousness. One's question may appear to be straightforward, but there may be deeper concerns, anxieties and motives underlying it; it is usually these that the Book will try to resolve. Then again, the actual language of the Book can be a challenge: in editions that are faithful to the original, the text is full of symbolism and poetic imagery, while other more modern editions may lack some of the original's subtlety and depth. So it takes practice and experience to become comfortable with the spirit of the edition that you have chosen to use.

This chapter, therefore, offers several examples of true readings that I have carried out either for myself or for others (who are of course anonymous). Well over half the hexagrams of the Book are represented. The wording of the question and the circumstances of the questioner are given, followed by the answer hexagram received. At this point, you are invited to consult the I Ching yourself and try to deduce what response is being given, by first identifying the trigrams, then reading the Judgement, then the text accompanying any moving lines, and finally looking for the result hexagram. If you wish, you could also identify and try to interpret the hidden nuclear hexagram.

The actual readings are then given so that you can compare your own thoughts with them and thus develop your skills of interpretation.

Enjoy the journey!

# LIGHTING THE PATH

## A. "Is it right for me to move back home?"

Adam is a student who had left home some time ago to be more independent and because, like many young people, he felt restricted by living with his parents. But his life had become more difficult and he wondered whether moving back home might offer greater calm and security; on the other hand, the original frustrations that caused him to move out in the first place could resurface...

The answer hexagram is 39: Obstruction. There is a moving line in the top place.

```
6  ── X ──
7  ─────────
8  ──   ──
7  ─────────
8  ──   ──
8  ──   ──
```

## A. The interpretation

The nuclear hexagram is 64: Before Completion, suggesting that in Adam's mind this is a very significant turning point as he contemplates a "transition from disorder to order". It is indeed a decisive moment and one that must be approached with very careful deliberation.

Hexagram 39 shows that Adam feels beset by difficulties and there seems no way to turn. But the trigrams describe the way forward. Below, there is Ken whose stillness tells him to pause for a while; sometimes when faced by challenges we just have to retreat (and in a real sense, moreover, that is what he did earlier by leaving the family home). Yet this is only so that we may be prepared to move forward again later when the difficulties pass, and the upper trigram K'an shows this energetic action ahead. The situation that he has found himself in has indeed been character-building.

There are even, perhaps, specific clues in the wording of the text that suggest the right direction to take: "join forces with friends" and accept "the leadership of a man", both of which phrases might refer to his parents.

The moving line in the top place is even more directly relevant. When faced with problems, sometimes it is understandable that one "turns one's back". But Adam should not take this approach, rather he is "called back... into the turmoil of life" – presumably, family life! Because of his experiences and personal growth, he will be able to achieve much and find "good fortune". The text further advises him to "see the great man", which means to accept the advice and authority of one who is wise and experienced – a parent perhaps?!

Confirmation is given by the resulting hexagram 53 : Development. The gentle, penetrating wind of Sun now stands above Ken's mountain, showing that difficulties can be steadily dispersed. An alternative image of Sun is that of a tree, firmly rooted. So Adam will find the security that he needs by returning to his family home. This hexagram often refers to family life, describing how good and happy relationships are created when those involved are adaptable and gentle, allowing matters to develop a step at a time.

## B. "Will I be successful in my job?"

Beth has recently started a new job. She feels that it is worthwhile but she doesn't seem to be making the progress that she hoped for. So she is wondering if she has made the right decision.

The answer hexagram is 9: The Taming Power Of The Small. There is a moving line at the top.

```
9  ——— o ———
7  —————————
8  ———   ———
7  —————————
7  —————————
7  —————————
```

## B. The interpretation

The upper trigram is Sun, the first daughter, whose attribute is the wind, and gentle penetration. The lower trigram is Ch'ien, the father, creativity and strength. So the image is that of the gentle wind blowing across the sky, restraining the clouds. Strength is being held back – release from trouble (the refreshing rain) is being promised but it is not yet the time...[18] Still, we can start preparing for it by acting with gentleness and friendliness, remaining very determined within while also refining our own nature.

The moving line at the top shows that in the upper trigram, the daughter, there is now movement. The top line of a hexagram shows what happens when a situation has now reached its peak and is changing. The text here shows that good character (of the female) has brought about a real difference and now is a time of rest and waiting. Beth must continue in what she is doing with gentleness, patience and caution, but she is also reassured that her work is indeed meaningful.

The resulting hexagram is 5: Waiting, or Nourishment. The upper trigram is now K'an, the second son, whose attribute is water. So the refreshing rain has now come. One must persevere (continue) in sincerity and inner strength, having the courage "to face things exactly as they are". In this way, great achievements are possible.

Sometimes we just have to accept that our efforts do not *seem* to be getting us very far (which is not to say that there is no progress). But here, because this hexagram *results* from the previous one, it represents a promise that the early

---

18 The text refers to the period in which King Wen, the modern father of the I Ching, was held in captivity. He created the I Ching hexagrams and wrote interpretations of them. Eventually he was released and his son Wu wrote the commentaries that we read today. So the hexagram is about being restrained by circumstances, but with the certain hope of good fortune later.

feelings of frustration *will* pass away, and that Beth will receive the nourishment (the rewards) that she hopes for. [19]

---

[19] So this result also refers to King Wen's release, which resulted not only in personal relief for him but in great spiritual nourishment for the whole world. This is a reading from the very heart of the I Ching.

# LIGHTING THE PATH

## C. "Should I follow my head or my heart?"

Charles is the manager of a company with a considerable number of people working for him, mostly women, with whom he has good relationships. He has to make a major decision about serious action to be taken soon. He understands both sides of the argument clearly. But while he is inclined towards one course, many of those who work for him disagree. His dilemma is perfectly expressed in the question!

The answer hexagram is 17: Following, with no moving lines.

```
8  ―― ――
7  ――――
7  ――――
8  ―― ――
8  ―― ――
7  ――――
```

## C. The interpretation

The nuclear hexagram here is 53: Development. This suggests that Charles' deeper concern is for the security of those he works with and for the good relationships that have been built up over time, because the hexagram describes the proper and cooperative relationships within the family, or between officials and others. Progress in the long term depends upon people's adaptability and care, and will only be undermined by hasty action or "any effort to exert influence on others". Intuitively, then, Charles already knows that he must not simply 'pull rank' in this situation.

The fact that there are no moving lines here indicates that there is indeed a clear and distinct decision to be made, and that the advice on the proper course of action is contained within the text of hexagram 17.

The lower trigram is Chen, who initiates movement and action; it is reasonable in this case also to think that he represents Charles himself. The upper trigram is Tui whose attributes are the joy and tranquillity that feminine energy brings to the world. Does she represent the workforce? We certainly see here the principles of masculine and feminine energy side by side – the head and the heart.

Delightfully, the text offers some very specific clues to Charles. "An older man defers to a young girl…" surely can be taken to refer to him and his (female) workers. Moreover, there is "Following has supreme success" and "In order to obtain a following one must first know how to adapt oneself… [and] learn to serve." Whenever one tries to lead merely by force, we are warned, there is bound to be resistance and all cooperation is lost. We must learn to adapt ourselves to the demands of a situation and be consistent in doing what is right – that is, "persevere".

# LIGHTING THE PATH

So Charles' answer is that to be a good manager he should defer, in this particular situation, to the feelings of those who work for him.

# LIGHTING THE PATH

## D. "How can I deal with my difficulty in trusting others?"

Dawn has had some bad knocks in life. She was abused while growing up and then, as so often is the case, went into a dysfunctional relationship and also suffered bereavement. She now finds it very hard to trust other people, especially when they get close to her.

The answer hexagram is 7: The Army, with the first, second, third and sixth lines all moving.

```
6  — X —
8  —   —
8  —   —
6  — X —
9  — O —
6  — X —
```

## D. The interpretation

The upper trigram is K'un, the Receptive, 'Earth mother' of the trigram family whose attributes are yielding, caring and perseverance; the lower trigram is the second 'son' K'an whose attributes are activity and water, often turbulent. The water here is below the Earth, thus the suggestion of hidden danger. In the context of this question, and because water also represents the flow of our emotions, the hexagram describes a situation in which Dawn's deep inner feelings are causing difficulties. There is 'agitation' below the surface and she has 'a fight on her hands'.

The I Ching uses the metaphor of an army to describe situations in which power needs to be assembled but in a very disciplined way, requiring clear and just aims and strong leadership. Without such unity, control and strength of conviction, armed force becomes chaotic, destructive and weakened.

Thus in our inner personal lives, too, we must identify clearly the challenges facing us (their nature and their causes) and focus our determination and intention, our spiritual and moral strength, on them. Yet we must be kind to ourselves, *engage the heart*, for nothing is achieved purely by force.

A 6 in the first place indicates that there must be "proper order". This line emphasises the comments above about the need for clarity about the issues and self-discipline in facing them. Right from the outset, Dawn must ask "Why is it that I have this difficulty? What has caused it, and how is it undermining my life now? Why must I do something about it?"

The moving second line refers to the "leader", the one who must take control in this situation. The leader is "in the midst of his army... equal to the heavy demands made upon him." As long as Dawn accepts some personal responsibility in this issue, both for perhaps playing a part in its cause and for being determined in addressing it, she can expect "good fortune". Her effort will be recognised by others i.e. will make a real difference in her relationships.

The third moving line is a difficult one and Wilhelm suggests that a mistranslation may be involved. But in any case, it does clearly suggest a warning: under no circumstances must one allow any outside interference in one's efforts. One's 'leadership' must be strong and determined, in not allowing either the influence of other people, or the nuisance of one's own 'inner demons', to deflect one from one's purpose.

The top line declares that "Victory is won". Dawn is assured that the difficulties (of trust) can certainly be overcome, bringing security and personal strength. Yet there is a further warning, to be resolute in having nothing to do with "inferior people". She must put a clear distance between herself and those – other people or situations – that do not serve her best interests.

Now, the situation referred to by the question is a very difficult one, and one that many of us face. It involves deep psychological and emotional forces. Thus, too, the answer must be considered with sensitivity. The comments above concerning responsibility in no way suggest that Dawn has brought her circumstances upon herself. But we must all recognise that we have a choice in how we respond to life's difficulties: do we continue to regard ourselves as unfortunate and helpless victims, or do we try to rise above "the slings and arrows of outrageous fortune" and to let go of the pain they cause? To be or not to be. It is certain that if we consider ourselves impotent in the face of others' mistreatment then we shall continue to attract to ourselves those people who would mistreat us and situations that could hurt us.

Dawn is being encouraged to analyse her experiences carefully and then to try and develop her personal strength and a determination to change her attitude of mistrust towards others. She must really be prepared to give others a chance, while being equally determined to have nothing to do with people who do not respect or care for her.

This is indeed challenging. But the resulting hexagram 22: Grace promises that it can be done. Here, the trigram of Fire is below the Mountain, suggestive of light breaking out into and giving beauty to the world. This can sometimes be an ambiguous hexagram, since such light is temporary and does not help to resolve major issues. However, in the context of this question, and because it is the *resulting* rather than the initial hexagram (and given the earlier moving lines), one can understand Grace for its spiritual meaning ~ a time of tranquillity and clarity when one is "removed from the struggle".

Dawn is reassured that the difficulties challenging her, and undermining her relationships with others, can certainly be overcome, yielding peace of mind.

Furthermore, the nuclear hexagram in this case also promises happier times ahead. It is 24: The Turning Point, describing a time when darkness is behind us and there is a natural transformation to lighter days. "The old is discarded and the new is introduced," and people come together in friendship. The ability to change the situation successfully is implicit in the question ~ the very fact that Dawn has asked it of the I Ching means that she wants to succeed.

# LIGHTING THE PATH

## E. "Should I change my job?"

Eden has been working hard on a certain project for a long time but no-one seems to be recognising his efforts. He is meeting with rejection and indifference, so is beginning to think that it may be time to move elsewhere or do something else.

The answer hexagram is 35: Progress, with the first and fifth lines moving.

```
7  ─────────
9  ───  O  ───
7  ─────────
8  ───   ───
8  ───   ───
6  ───  X  ───
```

## E. The interpretation

The trigrams are Fire over the Earth i.e. sunrise. This is a situation of expansion, of rapid progress. One who is in a dependent position is loyal to those above him. This brings great rewards. One should not allow one's purity of nature to become "clouded by earthly things". Clearly it is Eden who is in the dependent position here - or at least he feels that he is, because he is looking for others' recognition (which is the earthly thing). The I Ching suggests that this is not as important as the value of what we are trying to do, so the hexagram describes the attitudes that we should try to adopt when seeking to make progress under difficult circumstances.

The first moving line speaks of "Progressing but turned back" which is what Eden feels now. We may be concerned about others' rejection, the Book says, but the right thing to do is to continue doing what we know to be good, to stay calm and refuse to let a situation bring us down or lead to unhelpful emotions.

The moving line in the fifth place shows how the present situation will reach its peak. "Remorse disappears." One finds oneself in a position of influence and progress. It might seem that one is not making the most of it (of oneself) but this is unimportant – what matters is that one has opportunities to influence things for the good.

The resulting hexagram is 25: Innocence. The trigrams show strength of movement within Heaven, the effect of natural law. "Supreme success" when one is devoted to doing what is right, without ulterior motives or thoughts of personal advantage. In the spring time there is new growth. When one "surrenders innocently to the natural law", there is the possibility of unexpected helpful events.

So the reading promises success for Eden. And this may come about in an unexpected way, an idea suggested both by

## LIGHTING THE PATH

the fifth line (not making the most of oneself) and the resulting hexagram i.e. perhaps a promotion to a position that he hadn't considered before. He should stay where he is and persevere with his project to the best of his ability, not being concerned about any personal status. This attitude will be recognised and rewarded.

The nuclear hexagram here was 53 : Development, which is all about the proper and cautious procedures to be followed in seeking to achieve something worthwhile and to gain some kind of influence. This is exactly Eden's inner ambition and desire. One must not be precipitous or forceful if true and lasting effects are to be achieved. It is patience and perseverance that bring success, for things that are good and meaningful for us will come at the right time.

## F. "Will I find a happy relationship with a man in the next year?"

Fatima has been single for some time. She has had an active social life and has been a regular member of the party scene, but is now trying to move away from this because of its superficiality. She feels that her life is rather empty and she is lonely.

She cast hexagram 58: The Joyous, with moving lines in the second, fourth and fifth places.

```
8  ―    ―
9  ―  o ―
9  ―  o ―
8  ―    ―
9  ―  o ―
7  ―――――
```

## F. The interpretation

The nuclear hexagram, 37 Family, is telling in this case. It shows strong personal relationships as they should be, each person taking their proper role and responsibilities within the group in order to establish peace and security. Specifically, the relationship between husband and wife is highlighted as central (his strength, her loyalty and perseverance). This is what Fatima longs for.

Hexagram 58 represents a time and a situation of tranquillity, a gentleness in one's worldly affairs combined with inner strength and determination. This describes the attitude to be adopted in one's life in order to achieve joy. Much of the hexagram focuses on our relationships with others, and there may even be a specific 'clue' for Fatima in the words "Meeting with others for discussion and shared practice" – that is, she needs to get out and about, perhaps joining clubs or classes, in order to make new friends.

Indeed, all three moving lines here give very similar and consistent advice about letting go of her old life and old friends. In the second line we have "leave behind inferior people and inappropriate pleasures…" with the encouragement that if one's will is strong there will be no regrets about doing this. The fourth line again insists that she should make a clear decision to reject lower forms of pleasure and embrace the spiritual way if she is to find joy and peace. While on the way, the fifth line reiterates that she must have nothing to do with things or people that could undermine her progress. The Book's message could hardly be more clear.

If Fatima can follow this advice, the outcome is a happy one. Hexagram 24 is Turning Point, the time when 'darkness' and 'decay' are over and there is a natural transformation to new ways. The earlier 'clue' is also repeated: "People of like mind come together." There is indeed a meeting for her. In relation to the specific question, it is interesting to see here that the lower trigram is Chen, who arouses new activity and movement; he is of course also male, while the upper trigram is K'un, the archetypal woman.

# LIGHTING THE PATH

## G. "What is the future for my relationship?"

Greg described the relationship with his girlfriend as happy and meaningful, but quite often "challenging"... They'd known each for a few years, had broken up a few times but then always come back together soon after. "When it's good it's very, very good, but..." he said. They both recognised that they were learning a lot from one another and felt a sense of 'destiny' about being together. But their temperaments were very different, which caused arguments and misunderstandings on an everyday level.

Greg confided that he valued his partner highly, but often found himself longing for a more peaceful relationship!

His answer was hexagram 48: The Well, with no moving lines.

```
8  ──    ──
7  ──────────
8  ──    ──
7  ──────────
7  ──────────
8  ──    ──
```

## G. The interpretation

This is a truly spiritual hexagram, devoted to advising us how to live more meaningfully and make the best use of our material experiences. The structure of the trigrams suggests the form of a well, the source of essential life-giving nourishment, while their attributes describe the nature of the conscious individual. The lower trigram is Sun, who gently and thoughtfully penetrates to the inner meanings of life's situations, and perseveres despite difficulties; this describes one's attitude of mind. The upper trigram is K'an, fully involved in worldly activity. Thus the truly spiritual man or woman does not shy away from life and all its challenges, and seeks to learn and grow from the experience of being human by mindfulness and determination.

In ancient times (and still today in some less developed communities) the well was a central and highly important element of daily life for obvious reasons, and its structure hardly ever changed through the ages despite the massive social and political changes taking place around it. It stood, therefore, as a symbol of that which endures in human life, as well as its value in providing what is necessary to life itself.

Now, Greg's hexagram does not have any moving lines, indicating that his entire answer may be found in these symbols and images. While a good many of our ordinary and everyday activities exist on, as it were, the surface of life, every human being at times feels deeper needs (psychological, emotional and spiritual) that must be satisfied if he or she is to be content and wholly alive. We must reach down "to the very foundations of life". If we avoid or deny this imperative, or if we are careless in our attitudes to it, then we do not access the pure, life-giving spiritual energy that we need. (The image used in the Commentary is that of the rope not going all the way to the bottom of the well, or of the clay jug getting broken.)

So the hexagram warns us not to allow ourselves to be "fixed in convention": we must see beyond the superficialities of life and not be beguiled by the apparently 'easy life'.

Greg is being reassured that his relationship is genuinely meaningful and that he and his girlfriend are on a spiritual path together. They have had the good fortune to find in one another a true teacher, which is a pretty rare and joyful thing.

Whoever said that the spiritual way is meant to be easy?! Greg must honour this relationship to the best of his ability, and allow it to go as far as it can. Arguments and misunderstandings are sometimes (no, not always) simply the price we pay in the everyday world for the goods we receive in our inner world.

In human life we encounter and become involved in many different sorts of situations and relationships. Some of these are vital for our personal growth; others, while their effects are not so deep, are nevertheless important *practice*. Suppose I find myself having an argument with a rude and careless shop assistant. At one level, this is not too important because I may well never meet this person or visit that shop again. But I can learn something very important from this encounter (and indeed from every encounter in daily life), especially about the *choices* I have in responding to personal challenges. If I choose anger or confrontation, why am I feeling threatened? Alternatively, I could choose to realise that this is not so important and to let it go; or I could choose to feel compassionate towards the shop assistant, who may have his or her own serious personal difficulties...

So it may be that, in the long run, Greg's relationship will come to a natural end and he and his girlfriend will move onto other paths in life. But for now it is valuable and good (he said it is sometimes "very, very good") which is a matter of congratulation. On the other hand, there are times in life when however 'worthwhile' our experiences may be they are just too painful or we do not feel strong enough to stay in there. We should not beat ourselves up about this. There is no blame in having to walk away.

The lessons we needed to learn will come back later anyway!

## H. "What is the future for my relationship?"

Helena had been unhappily married but then later met a new partner and was very much in love. Their life together was good for quite a while until, as often happens, some important differences began to emerge between them which led to a 'trial separation'. Nevertheless, Helena felt that this would be temporary and that she would be able to win her partner back.

Her answer hexagram was 6: Conflict, with the sixth line moving.

```
9  ——— o ———
7  —————————
7  —————————
8  ———   ———
7  —————————
8  ———   ———
```

## H. The interpretation

Unsurprisingly, the nuclear hexagram in this case is 37: The Family, which focuses on the relationship between husband and wife as fundamental to the stability of human relationship. This is Helena's deepest concern and need.

In contrast to the previous example, where the trigrams were working together to produce an effect, consider that in hexagram 6: Conflict, we have Ch'ien above and K'an below. Heaven and water are two influences that are moving away from one another. Here, the word "conflict" does not have its everyday meaning; rather it describes a separation of people in the relationship.

The Judgement speaks of sincerity being obstructed and the need for inner strength; however good our intentions, sometimes things are against us and we have to fall back on our own psychological, emotional and spiritual resources because others' support is not there. It was in Helena's mind that perhaps the relationship could be healed, but the Book is unequivocal: "Going through to the end brings misfortune", and "Do not cross the great water", which is to say that however determined one may be to keep going there is no prospect of happiness, and one must not take any drastic action.

Yet the compassion of the I Ching is also evident in that advice is immediately offered on lessening the distress. "See the great man" urges Helena to seek professional help, perhaps from a counsellor. And it is vital, the Commentary goes on to say, that in such situations one must do all one can to reach a compromise with the other, acknowledging each other's needs and duties from the outset. We must not allow what is already an unhappy situation to descend into anger, bitterness and alienation.

How will this state of affairs turn out? As if reading Helena's mind (which of course it is), the I Ching then offers the top moving line. If one ignores the advice and still "carries on the conflict" – if Helena nonetheless does all she can to win back her partner – there may initially appear to a "victory". Yes, she could do this. But "happiness does not last" and there is "conflict without end". [20] The underlying energies are still pulling these two people apart.

The resulting hexagram in a reading usually presupposes that the questioner has understood and accepted the earlier advice given. In this case, however, it has already been implied that Helena is unlikely to do so. The I Ching therefore focuses here on reiterating its description of her true situation, while giving powerful spiritual encouragement. Hexagram 47 is Oppression (or Exhaustion – in the sense that one has lost the power to change things). In these circumstances, the Book says, you are oppressed and "held in restraint". It is a time of adversity. But if you can be strong despite the apparent personal 'danger', not allowing your spirit to be broken, this creates a stability and an inner power that will bring you good fortune – security, peace and happiness - in the future (for life's energies always do change).

Sometimes in life there is nothing one can do about one's situation. When we face serious personal challenges, the most important thing is to try and see things as they really are. To do this, and maintain one's integrity and self-respect, is the highest achievement of the spirit.

---

20 It didn't, and there was.

# LIGHTING THE PATH

## I. "How can I achieve financial security?"

Ian is a single parent. Through difficult personal circumstances, he had to give up his job in order to look after his child and has also had to move house to an unfamiliar area. Unsurprisingly, he is worried about his family's security. There is a possibility of work through an old contact but he feels hesitant about this, partly because the work itself does not seem at all meaningful. Yet he needs to earn money...

His answer hexagram is 25: Innocence, with the first line moving.

```
7  ─────────
7  ─────────
7  ─────────
8  ───   ───
8  ───   ───
9  ─── o ───
```

## I. The interpretation

The upper trigram is Ch'ien, the creative and fundamentally positive and light-giving principle, while the lower trigram is Chen, whose attribute is to arouse energy and incite movement in situations. Further, the first line of a hexagram represents that which is about to come into being, an energy in the hidden world that will soon manifest in change. This immediately suggests that an important new development can be expected in Ian's situation.

The hexagram as a whole speaks of a situation where there is "movement in harmony with the law of Heaven" – a *natural* course of events. This is also associated with the new growth of springtime, a period of creative activity coming after the darkness of winter when nothing seems to be happening. So Ian is being reassured immediately that there is an inner meaningfulness to his difficult life experiences, and that there is an underlying rhythm to our lives just like the seasons of the year. To appreciate this, and to remain calmly focused when times are bad, knowing that this will change, is the way of the Tao.

However, the Book insists (and this was stressed by Confucius in his Commentary) that this success can only come about when we are determined ("persevering") in following the spiritual way, surrendering to the natural flow of life's energies and being committed to being "the best we can be". Given this, we allow *entirely unexpected opportunities* to present themselves for our benefit. However, if we have ulterior motives, or a purely personal and self-interested agenda, things are not likely to go so well.

The first line strongly reiterates that if Ian is indeed set on a spiritual path, his *intuition* will be good and he can be assured of "good fortune" and the achievement of his aims (to establish security).

## LIGHTING THE PATH

The resulting hexagram is 12: Standstill, which normally describes a period of decline and disorder. However, this is clearly *inappropriate here*, given the strongly positive message of the original reading. Therefore we look in the Judgement for a specific and relevant message, and we find a powerful confirmation of the previous call to spirit: "...superior people do not allow themselves to be turned from their principles..." and "The superior man... does not allow himself to be tempted by dazzling offers to take part in public activities..." that involve "...assent to the meanness of others."

This is reinforced by the very structure of the hexagram, in which the two fundamental positive and negative principles are totally separated: a clear distinction has to be made by Ian between that which is positive, creative and life-affirming and that which is negative and undermining of his best interests. He must be very wary of any project that appears lucrative but is essentially "inferior".

Difficult though it certainly is in the circumstances, he should heed his intuition about the unsatisfactory work offer, reject it, and trust that life (destiny?) will lead him where he needs to go, to achieve not only financial security but personal growth as well. This may well be in the form of a quite unexpected opportunity, that is not as a result of any particular plans or ideas that he has in mind at present, or perhaps arising from an entirely new contact.

The I Ching truly understands our material issues and anxieties, but it also presents these to us in the context of their spiritual purpose. Ian is in effect being given a challenge. He has perhaps two possible paths to follow, one being the pursuit of material gain (for itself) and the other being dedication to the spiritual way of life. Paradoxically, it is *the latter* that is likely to bring the success sought after.

# LIGHTING THE PATH

## J. "What should I do to be more at peace?"

Jina is feeling very discontented with her life. She is middle-aged and feels that she has achieved little. Things don't seem to be working out well for her and she says that she has been "in a rut" for a long time. She is also in a relationship which does not satisfy her and she feels taken for granted.

The Book's answer is hexagram 63: After Completion. There are moving lines in the first and third places.

```
8  ──  ──
7  ──────
8  ──  ──
9  ──O──
8  ──  ──
9  ──O──
```

## J. The interpretation

The nuclear hexagram that reveals Jina's deeper concerns is 64: Before Completion, a metaphor for which is the springtime when the darkness and 'stagnation' of the winter is giving way to hopeful new life and growth. A "transition from disorder to order" is taking place ~ this is certainly what she is longing for.

Perhaps, too, she already feels intuitively that it is beginning to happen, for hexagram 63 describes just such a favourable time when "everything is in its proper place". Certainly, she does not know this consciously and there are perhaps no outward signs yet; but nevertheless our lives follow 'seasons' of change and sometimes we can feel the energies beneath life's surface that are bringing these about. Is this what prompted her to seek a reading now?

While this hexagram is the penultimate of the Book, it nonetheless represents a time of climax and a very significant turning point in one's affairs, nothing less than the end of an old cycle and the beginning of a new one. But one must not get carried away! It is vital to proceed with some caution – no hasty actions - and take care in all things so that the new ways can become established. These depend entirely on our having the right attitudes.

The first moving line re-emphasises this. There is definite change under way and it may happen quickly, taking one by surprise; it is really important that Jina checks herself and makes sure that whatever happens, and whatever others do, *her own behaviour is always correct*. Those who rush ahead thoughtlessly now are heading for a fall.

The moving third line goes on to describe the new situation when someone of great worth has now established order and security; this may refer to Jina herself who is now 'in control' of her own life. At the same time, there is a very clear warning that unworthy people, those "who have made themselves impossible at home" (!), must not be allowed to undermine things. So it is clear that Jina must distance herself from that bad relationship.

Given this, the resulting hexagram is 8: Holding Together, describing a time of security and harmony with others, being in the company of people with whom one feels at ease and can establish firm relationships.

This is a powerful and optimistic reading, yet as is so often the case it presents Jina with a challenge. Sometimes, at the very moment when we feel that we must *do something* and make changes, the proper thing to do is to hold back and trust in the way.

# LIGHTING THE PATH

## K. "I am being attacked. What will happen?"

Keith works in a caring profession and is very dedicated to his career. However, things have recently gone seriously wrong in a situation that he is involved with and he is getting the blame. He has examined his own position carefully and is quite sure that he has acted correctly. Nonetheless, it looks bad for him and there seems to be nothing that he can do about it.

The answer hexagram is 36: Darkening of the Light, with three moving lines, the first, second and sixth.

```
6  — X —
8  —   —
8  —   —
7  ———————
6  — X —
9  — O —
```

## K. The interpretation

The lower trigram Li is the second daughter of the trigram family, whose attribute is fire and the giving of light (enlightenment), warmth and nourishment; she is below K'un, the Earth, which of course extinguishes fire…This shows that someone who seeks to help and support others is being prevented, and is being personally wounded. The trigrams' positions also show how to behave in such difficult circumstances. The lower trigram represents one's inner attitudes: Keith must try to persevere in what he knows is right, maintain his spiritual integrity, keep his light burning; the upper trigram is the face that we present to the world - he must be yielding, quiet and modest, reserved in his dealings with others and trying to "let many things pass". This is going to be very hard!

The moving first line describes how this situation has started out. Keith is being prevented from making the progress he desires, and others misunderstand and even show ill-will ("gossip") towards him. Now, when our backs are to the wall yet we are determined to be true to our principles, stick to our guns ("he does not want to make compromises within himself"), then some suffering is unavoidable. However, this line also offers Keith support: "he has somewhere to go" means that he has a genuine personal destiny to pursue.

The second moving line speaks directly to Keith's integrity and encourages him in his work. "The injury is not fatal", the wounding he feels is not as bad as it might be – yes, it is painful but it can be healed. And if despite his difficulties he can still persevere in his job and try to help others who have been wounded in this situation ("saving the others who are also in danger"), good fortune will result from "acting according to duty". This suggests that not only can others' difficulties be resolved, but also Keith's efforts will be recognised. It

## LIGHTING THE PATH

is another challenge! When we are under fire, how hard is it to put others first?

But of course the I Ching goes further and guides us all the way through our situation. Note that the first two moving lines showed how the situation has begun, while the top line now shows that *it will pass away*. The 'darkness' and painfulness must reach a peak and will then be over with. Whatever has caused the wounding will not be able to do any more harm. So the situation will be resolved properly and those who are now attacking Keith will not be able to continue doing so.

The resulting hexagram is 18: Work On What Has Been Spoiled. Normally, the initial hexagram describes the present situation, the moving lines show the changes, and the resulting hexagram is the likely result of those changes. But in this reading, the result is reiterating the earlier situation while describing how it can be approached.

In hexagram 18, the still and powerful mountain confronts the gentle penetrating wind, which of course cannot move it. It is a situation of impasse, of wounding; but since it was caused *by the faults of others*, it is not irreparable, and the hexagram is all about how to deal with it. First, Keith must clearly understand those causes, and pause a while to gather himself. "Before the starting point, three days." Then he must move forward decisively and with determination to achieve what he has set out to do (to care for those others), on what he knows is the right way. He will be able to engage others' help in regenerating the situation, and achieve "supreme success" with "a new beginning".

It is again helpful in such a tricky case to look at the nuclear hexagram, which describes the deeper meaning of Keith's situation. Here it is hexagram 40: Deliverance. The deeper impulse behind the question is how to 'escape' from the dangers and difficulties he faces. This hexagram promises (in accord with the above top moving line) that 'deliverance' is now beginning and that he is entering a period when obstructions will be removed and problems resolved. It is a time of great change. The greatest challenge to us in situations where we are suffering injustice is to try and forgive others' failings and misdeeds, to wash the slate clean as soon as possible and then return to normal life.

# LIGHTING THE PATH

## L. "Will my studies be successful?"

Lorraine does not have a job because she has independent means. But she feels that she is not using her time productively; she is involved in several social activities that are quite enjoyable but she does not find them fulfilling. Therefore she is considering enrolling on an academic course, yet wonders if she is really up to it.

The answer hexagram is 17: Following, with the fourth line moving.

```
8  ──    ──
7  ─────────
9  ──  o  ──
8  ──    ──
8  ──    ──
7  ─────────
```

117

## L. The interpretation

The lower trigram shows the beginning of action and movement, while the upper is joyful. Because the 'son' defers here to the 'daughter' there is the sense of following in a humble and modest way. In order to grow and to gain understanding, so that we may have true influence in our lives, we must first accept the need to adapt ourselves to circumstances and *be prepared to learn from others*. The hexagram is associated with the Autumn-Winter period when there is increased darkness, a time when we should rest and take care of ourselves. Thus Lorraine is already being encouraged that her proposed course (and letting go of other activities) will be good for her, serving her personal growth and nourishment, as long as she is willing to involve herself fully in it.

The moving line in the fourth place emphasises that it is vital now to distance herself from all unnecessary and unhelpful attachments, especially people who may be attentive to her ("satellites") but only for their own "personal advantage". Such people are not genuine friends. Yes, her social activities may be enjoyable but now she should focus her mind instead only on what is important for her own development.

The resulting hexagram is 3: Difficulty at the Beginning. At first there is struggle, as energetic new life tries to force its way through the earth towards the air. Such difficulties are inevitable in the course of growth, rather like a child being born. But one should just persevere and stay involved, while also accepting that one cannot do everything on one's own.

Initially, things may seem unclear and unformed – taking on academic studies is daunting, involving new ways of thinking and considerable self-discipline - but order and a release of tension are implicit in the situation. Hence the promise of "supreme success", that is, being in harmony with the natural rhythm of one's life. Lorraine has to be aware that things are not likely to be easy, especially to begin with, and she may well go through a period of confusion that causes her to question her direction. So she should not hesitate to seek help from others when she needs it.

# LIGHTING THE PATH

## M. "Should I proceed with my project?"

Martin works in the media and is setting up an independent production company with a view to creating a particular artistic project. He is aware of the risks involved and that he will need others' collaboration. There are many uncertainties at this stage so he wonders whether the project is likely to be successful.

The answer hexagram is 26: The Taming Power of the Great, with a moving line in the second place.

```
7  ―――――――
8  ――   ――
8  ――   ――
7  ―――――――
9  ――― o ―――
7  ―――――――
```

## M. The interpretation

Hexagram 26 invites us to ask ourselves what our true motives are concerning the important situation we find ourselves in. It speaks of *the period of restraint before any future progress is possible*, thus suggesting that we take the long view... (It relates to the period of King Wen's imprisonment, when the strength of his forces was insufficient to free him from restraint. It is a time of *holding back* and nourishing what is really essential for our spiritual progress.)

This is a very significant undertaking for Martin ("cross the great water") but he is being advised to consider carefully before embarking upon it. The creative force is certainly there in the lower trigram, but it is held in check by the strength and stillness of the upper trigram. Much will depend on the clarity of his ideas and the strength of his personality as the leader in this project.

Moreover, there is a hint in the Judgement about the nature of the work involved: "not eating at home brings good fortune" means that "the worthy are honoured" to the extent that one accepts the Tao, the natural path of the spirit. Thus the project will succeed insofar as it is something that supports others (it is educational or uplifting) rather than merely self-serving (it promotes Martin's reputation or bank balance). He must stay connected to the Source and its guidance throughout. Further, he must "acquaint himself with many sayings of antiquity": some serious research is needed so that Martin knows his subject really well and is aware of what has been produced before.

These thoughts are emphasised in the moving second line. If the "axles are taken" from our car, there is nothing we can do about it but *submit to restraint*, to wait, until the proper time comes for advance when everything necessary is in place. It is not yet the time for Martin to proceed. 'Everything necessary' includes his own clarity of purpose and the work

## LIGHTING THE PATH

he must do on himself, just as much as the support (knowledge, skills, finance etc) required from others.

He has in mind a fine project so there is no reason to believe that this necessary support will not be forthcoming in due course. Yet the Book is asking him, before going any further, what his real motives are. Are they to honour those who will be the subject of the project or is this perhaps a commercial venture that serves other ambitions?

The two are of course not necessarily incompatible. If one is strong and clear-headed, with spiritual purpose, the right support and guidance, a most beautiful production can result. This is suggested by the resulting hexagram 22: Grace, which refers to things of artistic merit as well as of human value. But this hexagram also cautions Martin to be aware that, in this world, such things are not likely to have great impact ("small matters") or to be influential ("controversial issues").

This reading is not entirely optimistic is it? It neither promises success nor warns of failure. The reason for this is that it all depends on what Martin meant by the word "successful" in his question! Some light is shed on his inner state of mind by considering the nuclear hexagram, which is the tricky 54: The Marrying Maiden. While at one level this concerns the personal relationships between man and woman (see the next case), in other situations it counsels the need for "special caution and reserve" when proceeding with one's plans. One should not, here, seek personal influence but be prepared to take a back seat. Perhaps Martin is doubting his own ability to see this project through? Or is he unsure about the attitude that should be portrayed of his subject? "The superior man understands the transitory in the light of the eternity..." We should, if we want our work (and our lives) to be truly worthwhile, avoid all superficiality and instant personal gratification, and ensure that what we produce has true and lasting value.

# LIGHTING THE PATH

## N. "How will my love life develop?"

Nadia is a widow in late middle age. She is not lonely as such, and she has good friends, including men. But she misses the daily comfort and companionship of being married and wonders if the chance will come again.

Her answer is hexagram 54: The Marrying Maiden, with no moving lines.

```
8  ──    ──
8  ──    ──
7  ────────
8  ──    ──
7  ────────
7  ────────
```

## N. The interpretation

There is "thunder over the lake", the arousing (older male) is leading and the joyful (younger female) follows him. This represents a true relationship between man and woman. So this hexagram is clearly very appropriate to the question, but let's not get carried away with assumptions...

At the time that the I Ching was written, monogamy was normal but most marriages were matters of formal convenience and arranged between families. It was accepted that the man might have other intimate relationships and that his wife should even support this, even to the extent of welcoming the 'younger woman' into the household, albeit in a subservient position. So when this hexagram appears in relation to a more general question (as in the previous example), it describes a need for "special caution and reserve"; one must recognise one's lower status and not try to achieve undue influence, for this would lead to disorder and unstable relationships.

So what is this saying to Nadia, who is specifically asking about marriage? The Book is describing a situation in which there is true affection and union, which is of the greatest importance in all kinds of relationship. It is always important that we keep in mind what is good and true, that which endures, so that one doesn't drift away from natural paths or take wrong turns in life. But it may not be an 'official' relationship in the eyes of society. So Nadia will have such an informal relationship, a genuine source of happiness for her. And perhaps, since there are *no moving lines*, she already knows this person and their relationship will develop within their present situation.

The 'caution' mentioned suggests that she should not turn away from something that is good, satisfying and enduring, just because it does not quite fit with her desire for some kind of 'ideal' situation. When we insist upon the latter, it often turns out to be empty of real meaning. It is right to cherish and nourish what we already have that is good. [21]

---

[21] After the reading, she admitted that there was indeed a 'special man friend' in her life but for various reasons she did not believe they would ever be so close as to marry. A while later, the relationship developed...

# LIGHTING THE PATH

## 0. "My dream?!"

This is a most extraordinary 'reading'. Olivia is a middle-aged woman, recently retired from a very meaningful career and now rather unsure about the direction of her life. She needs to feel that what she does is purposeful. She has good friends but no special relationship, and she misses this.

Olivia attended two of my public lectures, the first about dreams and our ability to receive genuine spiritual guidance through them, and the second about the use of the I Ching. The night after the latter she had the following dream: "I was in an underground place; it was disused but full of stuff. It was a place where people could possibly look down into but I hoped they would not. All wrapped up with this somehow was the I Ching and I saw the number 38. This is a place of perfection and I was aware of the words 'solitude' or 'solstice' there... and then I knew that this was going to change into half of itself, number 19."

It seems that in her sleep Olivia was perhaps reaching deeply into her higher consciousness, well below the surface of the mind ("underground"). "...a disused place, full of stuff..." is pretty much a perfect description of that! Of course, it is also a very private place, so one doesn't really want others to look in there. Given that she had been to my lecture, perhaps she really was then unconsciously consulting the I Ching – without the Book even being present!

For hexagram 38: Opposition to change into hexagram 19, the fourth and sixth lines would have to be moving.

```
9  ——  o  ——
8  ——      ——
9  ——  o  ——
8  ——      ——
7  ——————————
7  ——————————
```

## 0. The interpretation

If we assume for the moment that this is indeed an I Ching reading, our next problem is that we don't know what the question was! But Olivia vouched safe that what had been much on her mind lately was the 'loss' of her career and her occasional feelings of loneliness.

To check on this, it is clearly appropriate to consider the nuclear hexagram, which reveals one's innermost thoughts. Here it is 63 : After Completion. It describes a time of equilibrium when everything is in the right place, one's efforts have come to fruition and there is a "transition from the old time to the new". It could hardly be a better metaphor for retirement from a lifelong career. But of course it is also common knowledge that many dedicated professionals fall into decline at such times, feeling 'unwanted' and not knowing what to do with themselves. Similarly, then, the commentary includes the warning that one must be careful in one's attitudes and not relax too much. Olivia seems to be worried, therefore, about how to use her new 'free time' with purpose.

It is surely also highly significant that the night of her dream was the autumn equinox, a significant turning point of the year when darkness starts to increase towards winter. In human terms, this may reflect feelings that life is slowing down, there is less growth, things aren't working out and one feels perhaps isolated (hence the word "solitude"). But those who are spiritually aware also know that there are rhythms and seasons in our lives, and are able to look forward and know that *everything changes*... So Olivia is also looking forward and reaching beyond this state to a time when growth will be renewed, to the next turning-point (hence the word "solstice"), and gaining inner strength in knowing that this period of 'darkness' will pass.

In hexagram 38 we see the trigrams of fire and water, energies that are divergent. Olivia is no longer sharing her life with those who think as she does, so she can achieve little; it is vital that she does not allow herself to be pulled down by superficial activities "with persons of another sort", but preserves her own individuality.

However, there is another side to this hexagram which might be telling here. 'Opposition' can also refer to the polarity of human life – Heaven and Earth, light and dark, man and woman – which is essential for creativity and vitality. In terms of close personal relationships she feels estranged, so perhaps it is this aspect of her inner anxieties that the reading is referring to?

We look to the moving lines for clarity, and both of them specifically describe a meeting with someone who will become important. The fourth line tells of a person who helps Olivia to emerge from her sense of isolation, someone who thinks in the same way as she does. The sixth line, which always represents the movement of one's situation into something new, suggests that she might indeed misjudge this person at first as unworthy; but then the misunderstanding is cleared up and she recognises him or her as a true friend. Their "union resolves the tension". While these comments seem to be in accord with the earlier remarks about personal relationships, it is wise not to be too literal. Rather than meeting with a person, it is possible that the Book is predicting – and this certainly seems to be a definite prediction – that Olivia will find some important activity or occupation that will be fulfilling.

So providing that Olivia can maintain her inner strength and focus on things that are worthwhile, her dream seems to be suggesting that the inner rhythm of her life is going to bring her renewal and happiness. The resulting hexagram 19 : Approach is all about the renewal of life-force, a time of joyful and hopeful progress, the approach of Spring *just after the winter solstice*. This was a profoundly optimistic and encouraging unconscious consultation!

# LIGHTING THE PATH

## P. "Will my new relationship continue to be good?"

Occasionally, one comes across a disturbing reading. With experience, one comes to trust the I Ching absolutely to pick out the true underlying energies of our lives and present us with real choices and wise advice. So when a reading throws up a suggestion of 'hidden deeds', one must be very cautious in handling the information!

If you do a reading for yourself but just don't understand the answer, then sit with it for a while but if it still makes no sense it's best to try again. If a reading for someone else is puzzling, that may be because you simply don't know enough about their circumstances – but they do.

Peter said that he was in a new relationship and that they were both very happy indeed. In fact, they had known each other for a long time before but could not be together because his partner had been married to someone else, who had now died. Could they possibly continue to be so happy, he wondered? (And I wondered why he needed to ask the question...)

The answer was hexagram 21: Biting Through, with the first and fifth lines moving.

```
7   —————————
6  ————  X  ————
7  —————————
8  ————    ————
8  ————    ————
9  ————  O  ————
```

## P. The interpretation

Because the question surprised me, I first looked for the nuclear hexagram which is 39: Obstruction. This describes circumstances in which one's progress is entirely blocked by "obstacles that cannot be overcome directly. In such a situation it is wise to pause…and to retreat." One needs to gather supportive friends and adopt an attitude of "unswerving inner purpose". In the present context this presumably refers to the fact that Peter had met his partner some time before but they couldn't be together then.

Hexagram 21 suggests that any such obstacles have now been removed, perhaps in some dramatic way, and there has been a sudden change in circumstances. (At one level, the hexagram often refers to legal actions; the text advises that strong action is needed but tempered by gentleness.) The inner trigrams represent the nature of the change: there is thunder and fire (lightning), the powerful force that makes things happen combined with the clarity of light. They may even, given the question, represent the two partners: one of strong and active character and the other gentler, a teacher of some kind who tries to bring nourishment to others. Either way, this relationship has an explosive character to it!

The moving first line, representing the very beginning of the relationship, shows that someone has suffered in some way and has been restrained. Is this Peter's partner? (In some cases there is also a warning associated with this line: there has been some improper behaviour and it must stop before it goes any further.) The moving fifth line looks ahead to the future development of the situation. It describes a time of difficult challenges when Peter must be acutely aware of his personal responsibilities and ensure that he is acting with utmost propriety (being "as true as gold").

One cannot escape the feeling that this reading holds a warning and that there is something disturbing that Peter needs to consider carefully; this is likely to show itself in future difficulties. If he faces these with a true heart then there will be "no blame".

But the hexagram that results is 12: Standstill, in which the male and female principles (the trigrams) stand apart. It is a further warning that if the difficulties are not faced and dealt with properly, there may be "disorder" and withdrawal.

Unfortunately, there does not seem to be a happy outlook for this relationship and one has to wonder whether at some level Peter intuitively knew that 'something is not right'. But only he and his partner could throw light on whatever that might be.

# LIGHTING THE PATH

## Q. "How will my life develop next year?"

Querida is a writer who believes passionately in the work she does. But so far she has met with little success. She has good friends and an active life but is single at the moment. At the turning point of the year we often review what has or has not been achieved, and look forward hopefully to the next twelve months. So this was a general 'New Year reading' – a straightforward request for predictions!

The Book's answer was hexagram 14: Possession in Great Measure. There were moving lines in the third and fourth places.

```
7  ─────────
8  ───   ───
9  ─── o ───
9  ─── o ───
7  ─────────
7  ─────────
```

## Q. The interpretation

Sometimes we may feel the need for guidance – there's some inner nagging instinct – but we are not sure what question to ask. In such honest circumstances it is perfectly acceptable to consult the I Ching anyway. Here, a question has indeed been phrased but even Querida herself doesn't quite know what she's asking.

This is where the nuclear hexagram can be especially helpful in reaching down to our important innermost concerns. In this case it is hexagram 43 : Breakthrough. This refers to times when "the inferior" begins to wane, tensions are relieved and there is a change to better conditions; one must be "resolute" in seeing this through. So after a frustrating period of little success, in her own eyes at least, Querida is hoping for some kind of breakthrough. The trigrams here have the attributes of creativity and joy, so in her case it would seem that it is her writing that is of greatest concern.

The I Ching then offers her reasons to be optimistic. Hexagram 14 is one of the most favourable in the whole Book, its trigrams declaring fire in Heaven, a bright light that illuminates things far and wide. These are propitious times when power is expressed with grace, bringing "supreme success". There is also reference to "wealth", although this is not necessarily meant to be understood in financial terms; happiness and personal success are indeed important forms of wealth in themselves. At the same time – we would of course expect it – the Book urges us to be modest in such circumstances and ensure that we use our 'great possession' to good purpose.

This theme is taken up by the third moving line, which reminds us that keeping good things just for ourselves is unworthy. But the significant words as far as Querida is concerned are, surely, that possessions should be placed "at the disposal... of the people at large." This can only be a reference, for a writer, to publication. The moving fourth line also talks about a rise in one's status (along with a further injunction to modesty!).

What is quite strange about this reading is that the resulting hexagram is 41: Decrease, which generally means exactly what it says. However, it does not necessarily mean something bad since both increase and decrease are natural in the rhythms of life, and we must learn to accept both with good grace. It is our inner attitudes that are more important than our possessions.

Nevertheless, this interpretation does not seem to follow on from the earlier very positive answer. In such cases, since we know that the I Ching is always entirely consistent, we should assume that the 'result' is an amplification of what has been said before, throwing further light on Querida's situation. It is undoubtedly true that she has been experiencing "a time of scanty resources". Hexagram 41 encourages us that such periods can indeed "bring out an inner truth" and enrich "the higher aspects of the soul", so the promised great improvements for her could be seen as a kind of 'reward' for her determined effort and her belief in the goodness of her work during those harder days.

The important lesson of this reading is that a resulting hexagram can *never* negate an answer hexagram, especially when the latter is supported by the nuclear hexagram. [22]

---

[22] Postscript: within the following year, through circumstances that couldn't possibly have been foreseen at the time of this reading, Querida's first novel was published.

# LIGHTING THE PATH

## R. "Will we get back together?"

Ron's girlfriend has uttered those terrible words "I need some space". They have had a stormy yet often very happy relationship for some years, but recent strains have taken their toll and she has decided that they should separate. Yet Ron loves her and still believes that they can have a future together, despite her words.

His answer is hexagram 62: Preponderance of the Small, with the fifth line moving.

```
8  ──   ──
6  ── x ──
7  ─────────
7  ─────────
8  ──   ──
8  ──   ──
```

## R. The interpretation

This is another example of the great value of the nuclear hexagram, because what Ron really needs to know is "what's going on under the surface of our situation?" Here it is hexagram 28: Preponderance of the Great. It is not so much the attributes of the trigrams that is telling in this hexagram as the image suggested by the lines: four strong lines with a weak line at either end is taken to represent the heavy ridgepole or central beam of a building that has insufficient support. It is therefore bound to collapse, "the load is too heavy" and things have got to be changed urgently. "It is necessary to find a way of transition as quickly as possible, and to take action." On the other hand, this is "not to be feared" and success is promised if Ron can only remain undaunted and adopt a gentle attitude in understanding the real causes of the situation – just why have things become too much for his girlfriend?

The rest of the reading is devoted to advising him how to conduct himself if there is to be a chance of reconciliation (which is his stated desire). Hexagram 62 reiterates the exceptional nature of the situation and his relative position of weakness. Again, it is the structure of the lines rather than the trigrams' attributes that gives the message. These are circumstances in which, for the moment, he cannot expect to achieve very much – nothing is going to change just yet. So he must examine his own feelings (a kind of bereavement) and ensure that the emotions he feels are genuine. Then, if he is still sure of his intentions concerning the relationship, he must behave with "exceptional modesty and conscientiousness": no strong actions or loud declarations are going to have the desired effect.

## LIGHTING THE PATH

The moving fifth line shows how the situation will develop and change going forward. Yes, there will be change. Ron is described in the commentary on this line as one who is "qualified to set the world in order" – that is, he is worthy – but needing others' help in carrying out "the exceptional task". There is a possible clue in a reference to this 'other' being one who has "withdrawn". He knew immediately who this might refer to – a good mutual friend who had tried to remain uninvolved and yet was very supportive of him.

So the Book's compassionate advice is clear. Ron must give careful thought to why his girlfriend found their relationship difficult and see things from her point of view. He must be constant in his care, and patient, and in the course of time ask their friend to mediate between them. This is a pretty tough challenge when one is feeling sad and lonely, and wants things to get back to how they were; it is particularly challenging to recognise that things cannot continue in the future to be as they were.

If he can do this, the outcome is very encouraging. Hexagram 31 is all about how we can influence others, with the secondary name of Wooing! The lower trigram is Ken, the calm and mature younger son, placed beneath Tui, the joyful daughter. The man acts with quiet modesty and consideration towards the woman, and thus attracts her (back) to him. This is the hexagram of peaceful and successful union, perhaps even of marriage. [23]

---

[23] It took four months, but it worked.

# LIGHTING THE PATH

## S. "I am being bullied at work. How should I deal with it?"

Sara enjoyed her work and felt that she had been doing a good job for quite a while; she had achieved good results and received praise. But when a new line manager was appointed, less qualified than her, he seemed to take an immediate dislike to her and started making things difficult. He made unreasonable demands, spoke unpleasantly to her and made false reports about her. So, almost out of the blue, her previously happy career became very distressing. Others advised her to take formal action but she hoped to avoid this.

The I Ching's response was hexagram 51: The Arousing, with the fourth and sixth lines moving.

```
6  ——  x  ——
8  ——     ——
9  ——  o  ——
8  ——     ——
8  ——     ——
7  ——————————
```

## 5. The interpretation

It is hardly surprising to find that the nuclear hexagram in this case is 39: Obstruction. One is faced on all sides by obstacles that cannot (yet) be overcome. "…it is wise to pause in view of the danger and to retreat." One can do nothing alone and must seek help. Anyone who has been in such a situation would hardly be comforted, either, by the Book's suggestion that it "is useful for self-development". Indeed, rather than blame others we should consider "the error within" ourselves and thus grow spiritually.

Tough advice! Of course, the I Ching is not suggesting that when others give us a hard time it is our own fault. But strength of character lies in our ability to recognise that there are always (at least) two sides to a story; we may sometimes inadvertently attract difficulties because we are not sensitive enough about how other people can respond to our words or actions. There is no blame in this. It's just life. But it is an opportunity for us to learn, if we have set ourselves on the path of trying to be 'the best that we can be'.

So at the core of this problem is a challenge to Sara. Can she try to understand why her line manager is treating her this way? What is it about *him* that causes him to react badly towards her (for example, feeling threatened or jealous)? And what is it about *her* that might provoke this (for example, aloofness or immodesty)?

The fact that the nuclear hexagram here is Obstruction, rather than, say, the apparently similar Opposition, is significant. In the latter we see two quite different personalities with divergent views, but not necessarily any enmity between them; they can still work together, up to a point. But here we have an aggression that stops us in our tracks and forces us to consider the underlying energies of the situation.

## LIGHTING THE PATH

The answer hexagram bears this out. The trigrams reveal thunder over thunder, a violent movement that produces shock and fear. But it is a force of *nature*, a "manifestation of God", and therefore has the ring of destiny about it. It has a purpose for Sara. At such times, "the superior man... examines himself... and searches his heart..." Am I being the best that I can be?

The moving fourth line describes a stalemate, where neither party is forcing the issue or showing signs of giving way. So there can be no movement. This is where Sara is now. The moving top line shows how the situation could change into something new, but it is another difficult challenge for her. When we are in shock, we lack clear vision; so the proper thing to do is to keep still and try to regain our composure. One who is able to withdraw from the issue "remains free of mistakes and injury". So Sara is being advised to do nothing and to let things go, otherwise she risks making things worse.

This is incredibly difficult to do, especially if we feel that a real injustice is being done. And of course this would not be the Book's advice in every situation of conflict. But these are circumstances, it seems, in which she cannot 'win'.

On the other hand, there is still much for her to gain, for the resulting hexagram is 27 : Nourishment. If she can accept the earlier advice about introspection and letting go, she will be cultivating the superior parts of her nature. There can be true spiritual growth if one can be moderate in one's actions and tranquil in one's words.

Ф

However, Sara felt deeply wronged at work and dissatisfied by this reading. A little later, she insisted on the follow-up question:

> "What would be the outcome of making a formal complaint?"

The answer hexagram was 59: Dispersion with a moving fifth line.

This is so brilliantly appropriate. Firstly, note that Sara is essentially asking *the same question as before*, because taking action was already in her mind. She is just making the thought more explicit now. So it is not surprising to find that the nuclear hexagram here is again 27 : Nourishment, the same as the previous answer hexagram. We thus have a genuine follow-on.

We also note that the spirit of the Book is kind, recognising how difficult it is to accept the advice given earlier. Hexagram 59 therefore reiterates that the problem can only be overcome by gentleness and spiritual attitudes. (The upper trigram Sun is the wind that gently disperses the lower K'an's energetic water. When one's energy is dammed up, "gentleness serves to... dissolve the blockage.") The moving fifth line declares that "a great idea" brings about salvation and recovery; this idea was expressed already in the first reading, the encouragement to adopt a spiritual attitude, to be great.

But at this point, the Book's patience runs out. Its spirit does not like to be asked the same question twice, so the resulting hexagram is 4 : Youthful Folly. "The young fool seeks me. At the first oracle I inform him. If he asks two or three times, it is importunity."

This is invariably the result if we ask superficial questions or those implying doubt in the advice already given. When we ask the I Ching a question, we reach into our deepest mind and receive the answer. If that is clear, yet we ask substantially the same question again, what different answer can be given? Sara was fortunate to be given a reminder of her answer, before being told to go away.

# Appendices

# Appendix A   On Probabilities

If there is to be a true *synchronicity* between our unconscious mind, the conscious question asked, and the physical method of consulting the I Ching, then clearly that method must be a genuinely *random* one, beyond our conscious influence. If we are careful with the methods described in this book (for example, by shuffling the cards thoroughly) then all of them are so.

But there is another pertinent issue. Should the method adopted also be mathematically *fair* – that is, should there be an equal chance of choosing yin or yang? If this is not so, then some outcomes are going to be more likely than others. In turn, this means that when we ask a question some answers will be more likely than others. But surely we want the fullest possible range of answers available to us?

In the chapter on Methods, I mentioned the argument put forward by some that this apparent problem is not important. On the one hand, it is said, our unconscious minds will be able to take the imbalance into account and still provide us with true responses. It has also been suggested that the imbalance is *natural*, because it is in the nature of yang to 'move' while yin prefers to be yielding and 'at rest'; therefore we should expect moving yang lines to occur more frequently than moving yin lines (which is the case with the Yarrow Stalks and Marbles methods).

You must decide for yourself whether such an argument is convincing or not. In this Appendix, I shall show the basic methods of calculating the probabilities of the various outcomes for all the consultation methods described in this book. Don't panic! If you don't like Maths you can turn over to the Conclusions at the end of the chapter.

In the following calculations, p( ) means the probability of the event in brackets. For example, p(yin) means the probability of the outcome being a yin line. The value is always a fraction between 0 (impossible) and 1 (certain).

# LIGHTING THE PATH

## Yarrow Stalks Probabilities

In **Step 2**, the possibilities are as follows:

| R | 1 | 2 | 3 | 4 | 5 | etcetera | 47 | 48 | |
|---|---|---|---|---|---|---|---|---|---|
| L | 48 | 47 | 46 | 45 | 44 | etcetera | 2 | 1 | |
| R | 1 | 1 | 1 | 1 | 1 | | 1 | 1 | ) |
| E | 4 | 3 | 2 | 1 | 4 | | 2 | 1 | ) the remainders |
| S | 0 | 1 | 2 | 3 | 4 | | 2 | 3 | ) |
| U | | | | | | | | | |
| L | n/a | =3 | =3 | =3 | =2 | | =3 | =3 | (3 = yang, 2 = yin) |
| T | | | | | | | | | |

3 occurs 36 times out of 47, and 2 occurs 11 times,

so p(3) = 0.766 and p(2) = 0.234 to 3 decimal places.

**Step 3**: if the Step 2 result was 3, leaving 44 stalks, the possibilities are:

| R | 1 | 2 | 3 | 4 | etcetera | 43 | |
|---|---|---|---|---|---|---|---|
| L | 43 | 42 | 41 | 40 | etcetera | 1 | |
| R | 1 | 1 | 1 | 1 | | 1 | ) |
| E | 3 | 2 | 1 | 4 | | 1 | ) the remainders |
| S | 0 | 1 | 2 | 3 | | 2 | ) |
| U | | | | | | | |
| L | n/a | =3 | =3 | =2 | | =3 | (3 = yang, 2 = yin) |
| T | | | | | | | |

3 occurs 22 times out of 42, and 2 occurs 20 times,

so p(3) = 0.524 and p(2) = 0.476 to 3 decimal places.

But if the Step 2 result was 2, leaving 40 stalks, the possibilities are… etc. The full mathematical calculation is available from the author.

## Marbles Probabilities

If there are 38 marbles (or discs) altogether:

11 represent yang lines so p(yang) = 11/38 = 0.289 to 3 decimal places

17 represent yin lines so p(yin) = 17/38 = 0.447 to 3 decimal places

8 represent moving yang lines ...... etcetera

## Coins Probabilities

When a coin is tossed the probability of each face is 0.5 and when three coins are tossed their probabilities are multiplied together.

p(6 or moving yin) = p(9 or moving yang) = 0.5 x 0.5 x 0.5 = 0.125

p(7 or yang) = 0.5 x 0.5 x 0.5

but this is multiplied by 3 because it can happen in 3 ways (223, or 232, or 322)

so the probability = 0.375

p(8 or yin) is the same.

## Playing Cards Probabilities

There are 26 red and 26 black cards, so if cards are not replaced after being chosen the probabilities are as follows:

p(6 or moving yin) = p(9 or moving yang)

= 26/52 x 25/51 x 24/50 = 0.118 to 3 decimal places

p(7 or yang) = 26/52 x 25/51 x 26/50 for red/red/black but then it's the same total for red/black/red and for black/red/red so the probability = 0.382 to 3 decimal places

It's the same result for p(8 or yin).

# Personalised Cards Probabilities

In the first example given, a set of cards is made up composed of two types, one representing yang (value 3) and the other yin (value 2). Three cards are then chosen and their values added. But the results obtained will depend on the number of cards in the set.

If there are **Six** cards (3 of each) which is the minimum number:

p(6 or moving yin) = p(9 or moving yang) = 3/6 x 2/5 x 1/4 = 0.05

p(7 or yang) = 3/6 x 2/5 x 3/4 = 0.15 for yin/yin/yang, then it's the same total for yin/yang/yin and for yang/yin/yin, so the probability = 0.45

It's the same result for p(8 or yin).

If there are **Twenty** cards (10 of each):

p(6 or moving yin) = p(9 or moving yang) = 10/20 x 9/19 x 8/18 = 0.105

p(7 or yang) = p(8 or yin) = 10/20 x 9/19 x 10/18 but this can occur in three different ways, so the probability = 0.395 (results to 3 decimal places).

# Short Cut Cards Probabilities

Only one choice is made from the eight cards for each line of the hexagram.

p(6 or moving yin) = p(9 or moving yang) = 1/8 or 0.125

p(7 or yang) = p(8 or yin) = 3/8 or 0.375

## Conclusions: Yarrow Stalks Method

p(6 or moving yin line) = 0.052 ;  p(7 or yang line) = 0.289;

p(8 or yin line) = 0.448 ;  p(9 or moving yang line) = 0.211

(all to 3 decimal places).

The mean (average) number of moving lines per hexagram is 1.578

But a yin line is 1.6 times more likely than a yang line, and a moving yang line is 4.1 times more likely than a moving yin line. So this method is random but **not** mathematically fair.

## Conclusions: Marbles Method

p(6 or moving yin line) = 0.053 ;  p(7 or yang line) = 0.289;

p(8 or yin line) = 0.447 ;  p(9 or moving yang line) = 0.211

(all to 3 decimal places).

The mean number of moving lines per hexagram is 1.584

This replicates the Yarrow Stalks Method so again is not mathematically fair.

## Conclusions: Coins Method

p(6 or moving yin) = p(9 or moving yang) = 0.125;

p(7 or yang) = p(8 or yin) = 0.375

The mean number of moving lines per hexagram is 1.5

Yin and yang lines are equally likely, as are moving yin and moving yang lines, so this method is both random and mathematically fair.

## Conclusions: Playing Cards Method

p(6 or moving yin) = p(9 or moving yang) = 0.118;

p(7 or yang) = p(8 or yin) = 0.382   (figures to 3 decimal places).

The mean number of moving lines per hexagram is 1.416

Yin and yang lines are equally likely, as are moving yin and moving yang lines, so this method is both random and mathematically fair.

## Conclusions: Personalised Cards Method

For **6** cards, p(6 or moving yin) = p(9 or moving yang) = 0.05;

p(7 or yang) = p(8 or yin) = 0.45

These probabilities show that the method is mathematically fair.

However, the mean number of moving lines per hexagram is only 0.6, less than half that for the previous methods, which is unsatisfactory.

For **20** cards, p(6 or moving yin) = p(9 or moving yang) = 0.105 ;

p(7 or yang) = p(8 or yin) = 0.395

Again, we have equal probabilities so the method is mathematically fair.

But the mean number of moving lines per hexagram is still only 1.26.

In fact, it can be shown by continuing with the calculations given earlier that we need **46** cards for the mean number of moving lines per hexagram to reach 1.4 and *it is not possible* by this method to achieve 1.5 moving lines per hexagram, as with the Yarrow Stalks or Coins methods.

## Conclusions: Short Cut Cards

p(6 or moving yin) = p(9 or moving yang) = 0.125;

p(7 or yang) = p(8 or yin) = 0.375

Equal probabilities means that the method is mathematically fair.

The mean number of moving lines per hexagram is 1.5.

## An Experiment

Finally, it may be thought that theoretical Mathematics has little to do with a psychic (if not mystical) event such as consulting the I Ching. Therefore, I have carried out a practical examination of actual consultations to compare with the above results. The findings are very interesting.

I looked at sixty-four consultations using the Coins method carried out during a period of fifty months.

There were 47 moving yin lines and 51 moving yang lines, with an average of 1.531 moving lines per hexagram. These results are almost exactly as predicted by the Mathematics above.

| # of moving lines | 0 | 1 | 2 | 3 | 4 | 5 | 6 | |
|---|---|---|---|---|---|---|---|---|
| Frequency | 10 | 27 | 18 | 3 | 4 | 2 | 0 | [σ = 1.19] |

For example, 10 hexagrams had no moving lines at all, 27 hexagrams had just one moving line, and so on. The distribution has a positive skew as would be expected (since the mean number of moving lines is about 1.5), but the results suggest that the method is genuinely random and fair.

# LIGHTING THE PATH

HOWEVER... if the exercise were *purely* random then one would expect an even distribution of actual hexagrams i.e. each hexagram occurring roughly an equal number of times. Ten consultations yielded no moving lines, so there were 118 hexagrams occurring in this experiment.

| Frequency of occurrence | 0 | 1 | 2 | 3 | 4 | 5 | |
|---|---|---|---|---|---|---|---|
| # of hexagrams | 9 | 20 | 17 | 9 | 8 | 1 | [σ = 1.29] |

Thus nine of the Book's 64 hexagrams never occurred at all, twenty of them occurred just once each... and nine hexagrams occurred four or more times.

*This clearly suggests that there IS some 'other factor' determining which hexagram is generated in a consultation ~ presumably its meaningfulness in relation to the question!*

# Appendix B  The I Ching's Attitude to this Book

I wanted to write this book because I felt that other titles did not give sufficiently clear and straightforward explanations, especially for those who are new to the I Ching, for everything involved in getting to know the Book and how to use it. There are indeed many other excellent titles that go into greater depth, but they can be rather technical. Moreover, there are not many actual examples of readings given to help one develop skill in interpretation.

However, I am not an academic expert on the I Ching and I am very much aware that there are many others more skilled than me. Therefore it felt right that I should consult the I Ching myself – as I tend to do with all important decisions – about the wisdom of embarking on this book. The result was both fascinating and cautionary!

> "I want to write a short book to help others learn how to use the I Ching. Is this a good idea and will it be successful?"

```
8  ——  ——
9  ——  o  ——
9  ——  o  ——
8  ——  ——
8  ——  ——
7  ————————
```

This is Hexagram 17: Following, with the 4th and 5th lines moving.

The lower, or inward, trigram is Chen, the Arousing. In this situation I am wishing to make things happen, to get a project started, and there is strong energy in my thoughts and ambition. The upper, or outward, trigram is Tui whose attribute is the joyfulness that follows her older sister's gifts of enlightenment and the warmth of human contact. Yes, I am hoping to reach out to people and shed some light on this very Book. And, in a sense, I am trying to gain a kind of 'following' for my own writing.

At this point it is pertinent to look also at the 'hidden' nuclear hexagram which can reveal one's deeper motives or possible unexpected dangers in the situation. Here, it is Hexagram 53: Development. This speaks of good fortune and progress, but a need to proceed very cautiously step by step always with regard to proper relationships. Moreover, any attempt to "exert influence on others" must be sensitive and thoughtful, based on careful attention to my own "moral development". Thus I am being warned (and this will be reiterated in Hexagram 17) not to rush into the project perhaps thinking it will be easy, but to take my time ensuring that it is done thoroughly and with a proper relationship to the I Ching itself. I took this to imply humility.

## LIGHTING THE PATH

Returning to Hexagram 17 now, the Judgement promises "supreme success" which means that the idea is in harmony with the natural rhythm of life. But this comes with a stark caveat: "In order to obtain a following one must first... learn to serve..." In other words, if my book is to be at all worthwhile, I have first got to make sure that I know what I'm talking about! I must do deeper study of the Book yet and "persevere" with this learning. The hexagram is associated with the time of autumn and with the need for a season of proper rest.

So I did as I was told and set about developing my understanding of the I Ching both by reading others' works and by carrying out consultations, discovering that I did indeed have a lot to learn! This book was written in the dark days of late autumn and, yes, I found that it's surprisingly tiring to live and work at the edge of inner consciousness... The moving lines re-emphasised the moral advice I had already noted.

*9 in the 4th place:* One must be entirely free of ego and intent only on doing what is right and essential, disinterested in any superficial following one may have. So this book must be written for its own sake and to the best of my ability, irrespective of whether it is 'commercial'.

*9 in the 5th place:* As long as the book is written with true conviction, as a 'labour of love' for what is good and beautiful, there will be good fortune.

The I Ching had thus looked deeply into my eyes (and my soul) and suggested, quite kindly I think, that if I were to be so presumptuous as to try and write yet another book about it, things would turn out all right as long as I went about it seriously, with humility, understood the great responsibility of what I was attempting, and learned more about my subject than I thought I already knew……

The resulting hexagram was one of my favourites, number 24: Return. This describes a time when there is a natural transformation from a period of darkness (a lack of understanding) to the light. This is exactly what I was hoping to achieve, helping others to begin their own relationship with the I Ching. The trigrams describe thunder within the earth, the movement of new energy as the approach to springtime begins. (The book was finished just after the winter solstice and published in early spring.) People "with shared values and interests" will now come together – I think that means you!

# Appendix C   A Glossary of Words and Phrases

These are some of the most common or important words and phrases used in the I Ching, with a description of their meanings. The word 'I' itself means both change and our response to how things are transformed; 'Ching' means The Classic Book.

# Principles

| | |
|---|---|
| **The Dark** | A state of confusion or misunderstanding; a weak position. |
| **Earth** | Everything that is of the natural world as humans experience it, all that is receptive and persevering and is of the Earth. This is *Yin*. |
| **Evil** | That which leads to darkness, or undermines the natural path. |
| **Fate** | The patterns of events in our lives, and their outcomes, which result from our own actions and decisions. |
| **God** | The highest state of being, true spirituality. |
| **The Great** | That which is strong and creative, holding things together, an action based on conviction. However, that which is too strong can be overpowering. |
| **The Great Man** | A source of spiritual wisdom and advice. It may be a person, one with influence and strength, an expert. It may represent the emergence of our own highest Self. It may be the I Ching. |
| **Heaven** | Everything that is of the spirit, that is light and creative, the primal energy that moves in the unseen world, is of Heaven. This is *Yang*. |
| **The Light** | A state of understanding and strength, in harmony with the Tao. |

| | |
|---|---|
| **Realising** | One who is genuinely following the spiritual way, whose life is in harmony with the spirit of change, is a realising person. |
| **The Small** | A (temporary) situation in which little can be achieved; we must simply be patient and do whatever we can, being adaptable to the circumstances. |
| **Spirit(s)** | The unseen forces that shape our experience. Originally thought to be gods, demons, ghosts, ancestors etc, we now understand this as the human unconscious; strength and creativity can inspire us, while ill-feeling and past wounds can hinder us. |
| **Strength** | Active, creative energy; of the light and the spirit. The Yang is strong. |
| **Sublime** | In harmony with Heaven's will, with the greatest good. |
| **Success** | Staying in harmony with one's natural path and thereby making personal and spiritual progress. |
| **Superior Man** | A person who seeks to be true to the Tao, and to be the best that he or she can be in harmony with the inner self. The Superior Man accepts the wisdom and advice of the I Ching. By contrast, the *Inferior Man* is the voice of the ego, of limited self-interest, of self-protection irrespective of what is spiritually right. |

| | |
|---|---|
| **Tao** | The natural path, the rhythms of nature; an individual's Tao is the path of their life that is in harmony with natural forces and consistent with their true inner nature. This is the spiritual way. |
| **Virtue** | A measure of one's personal strength and development on the Tao. With virtue one is becoming one's true self, and with it one influences others. |
| **Weakness** | Passive and receptive, devoted and persevering; of the Earth. The Yin is weak. Weakness is not a pejorative word. |

# Images

| | |
|---|---|
| **3 days** | A period of caution and thoughtfulness. |
| **10 (or 7) days/yrs** | A natural cycle of time. |
| **Bull, boar** | Wild and aggressive forces. |
| **Cow** | Docility, reticence; something to be cared for. |
| **Dragon** | That which is strong, active and creative. |
| **Fish** | Those who are Followers; insignificant people. |
| **Fox** | One who tries to gain undue influence by insinuating himself with those of authority; one who manipulates others. |
| **Goat** | The impulse to push forward thoughtlessly. |
| **(Wild) goose** | One who is faithful to his path, and to others. |
| **Hamster** | One who is dishonest or attracted to the superficial. |
| **Hawk** | That which is to be hunted, a powerful but dark influence that must be brought down. |
| **Horse (mare)** | Perseverance with strength and modesty. It is also given as a reward. |
| **Pig** | Stupid and intractable people. |
| **Tiger** | People or situations that are strong and beyond our control. |

| | |
|---|---|
| **Tortoise** | One who is spiritually evolved, free of Earthly concerns. It is also a symbol of the Oracle. |
| **East, north** | A time and a place of retreat, of quiet and introspection. |
| **West, south** | A time and a place of energetic activity, where we find Helpers. |
| **Black, dark blue** | The colour of Heaven and of all that is strong. |
| **Gold** | Truth. Strength. |
| **White** | Simplicity, purity of mind. |
| **Yellow** | The colour of Earth and all that is weak; impartiality, the middle way; in line with one's duty and that which is correct. |

## Conditions

**Abyss, Abysmal** — A situation in which one's sincerity and strength of character are being challenged.

**Adversity** — A time of suffering or personal danger, often resulting from past situations; its causes must be understood and its effects confronted.

**(take up) Arms** — Taking deliberate action against anything that undermines the Light and our true nature; this may be other people's behaviour, or our own inferior nature and habitual behaviours.

**Completion** — A time when everything seems to be in its proper place, and is therefore bound to change.

**Conflict** — A situation in which two or more forces or impulses are taking us in different directions. The Book advises several alternative ways of resolving this depending on the circumstances. But Conflict can also represent the natural duality of human life (of Heaven and Earth, of spirit and nature, of man and woman) which can be essential to our growth and not necessarily to be avoided.

**Cross the great water** — To go ahead with difficult or challenging projects and activities, to persevere despite opposition, knowing that it is the right course.

| | |
|---|---|
| **Decoration** | Some kind of reward or recognition for one's effort. |
| **Disperse** | To dissolve away gently any forces or personal impulses (ego) that might undermine our progress on the natural path. |
| **Endure, Duration** | An attitude or situation that is natural and strong, in accord with the times. It does not imply, of course, that the situation will continue without change. |
| **Following** | Not pushing forward, not making active decisions, but being quiet and allowing oneself to be guided by the inner voice (or by others). |
| **Fool, Foolishness** | Immaturity, inexperience, lack of wisdom. |
| **Furthering** | Making progress on one's natural path; promoting the spiritual way in all things and for all people. |
| **Helpers** | Any kind of support we receive that is in harmony with the Tao. It may be of our own inner strength and wisdom, or it may be other people who are acting with us for the highest good. |
| **Humiliation** | A situation of regret or sorrow, usually through having lost touch with the natural way by wrong actions or attitudes. |
| **Innocence** | A state of modesty, of acceptance of the Tao. This also implies the possibility of unexpected or surprising events. |

| | |
|---|---|
| **Keeping still** | Deliberately quietening the ego so that the inner voice of the higher self, of wisdom and clarity, may be heard. |
| **Modesty** | The highest virtue; the way of the Superior Man. |
| **Nothing furthers** | No good will come of this approach or action. |
| **Nourishment** | Anything that gives strength or is in harmony with nature, from good food to understanding to spiritual guidance. |
| **Oppression** | A time of adversity when dark forces have influence and one's progress is held back. |
| **Penetration** | A gradual process of understanding and personal growth, in contrast to *Pressing forward* which can often be the way of ego. |
| **Perseverance** | Tireless strength and devotion to the Tao, and acceptance of one's dependence on others and on the guidance of the Spirit. However, this does not imply inactivity, rather that we achieve things by learning what is required of us by a situation. |
| **Sacrifice** | Engaging in spiritual practice, letting go of 'the Inferior Man' for the highest good. |
| **Stillness** | Not inactivity, but a quietness of heart and a willingness to live in the moment. |
| **Union** | Forces that are naturally coming together to complement one another. |

**The Well**    Symbol of the true Source of spiritual strength, wisdom and guidance that never changes. It is within each of us and it is here that we must go if we sincerely seek the Tao and to be all that we are capable of being.

# Bibliography

This is just a brief list of excellent translations of the I Ching.

*I Ching, or book of changes*
Richard Wilhelm, Cary F Baynes (1951)

*I Ching, The Book of Change*
John Blofeld (1965)

*I Ching, A New Interpretation For Modern Times*
Sam Reifler (1974)

*A Guide To The I Ching*
Carol K Anthony (1980)

*How To Use The I Ching*
Stephen Karcher (1997)

*The Complete I Ching*
Alfred Huang (1999)